GREAT
IN RACING

EDITED BY
TONY MORRIS

Nearly New 3/,

Mose. Tosci

Stirling Castle.

QUEEN ANNE PRESS, LONDON

Cover photo: Grundy winning the King George VI & Queen Elizabeth Diamond Stakes at Ascot, July 26 1975 (see story in Chapter 14). *Photo courtesy of Syndication International.*

Published by Queen Anne Press Limited
12 Vandy Street
London EC2A 2EN

Printed and bound in England by
C. Nicholls & Company Ltd.,
The Philips Park Press, Manchester

CONTENTS

FOREWORD

Racing has held such an overwhelming fascination for all sections of the community over two centuries that it has long been the best documented of all popular sports. Someone who, like myself, enjoys researching into Turf history as well as trying to keep abreast of current developments, knows only too well the vast amount of literature it has inspired. When the space to accommodate a racing library dictates your choice of home, you appreciate the scale.

I would therefore be the last person to add to this phenomenally extensive range, even with this modest offering, unless it seemed to fill a genuine need. I hope and believe that it does. Too many books devoted to Turf history merely repeat or rehash familiar stories from earlier volumes, many of which were erroneous in the first place; too little original research is conducted at the most reliable source, the contemporary sporting Press. Although all the facts contained in *Great Moments in Racing* have long been public property, many have never appeared before in book form.

The choice of 'moments' was purely arbitrary – occasions which appealed to me as a writer and as an enthusiast. They were not selected with the intention of trying to persuade the reader that these 14, above all others, deserve to be recalled. By the same token, while all (with the obvious exception of Aboyeur's Derby) revolve around races won by horses who have or had some claim to be regarded as 'great', the subjects do not form my idea of the 'greatest', although my enthusiasm for some will no doubt prove readily apparent.

I embarked on this book only a few weeks after attending the last great moment it describes. I returned home stimulated by the firm conviction that I had been in the presence of greatness – one of the most invigorating and comforting feelings I know – and inquired of my partner whether she had seen it on television.

'Was that the one with Grundy in it?' The implications of her reply did not hit me for a moment and I followed up at once with, 'Yes, and wasn't that the most exciting race you have ever seen?'

Back came the stunning, deflating logic I should have expected.

'Well, the last bit was exciting, but all the first part was very boring, wasn't it?'

I was quite unable to produce an adequate response at the time, but I kept her devastating remark in mind when I wrote what follows. And, believe it or not, she liked it.

I hope you do too.

TONY MORRIS

THE FLYING DUTCHMAN

*when half a county turned out to witness a unique match
between two Derby and St Leger winners*

In the early part of the seventeenth century, when the sport
of kings first began to flourish under the patronage of Charles
II and his court, there was virtually only one kind of race –
the match. The contest concerned only two horses, 'matched'
by their owners to determine relative merits and to effect a
certain redistribution of wealth, sometimes with the weights
adjusted in an effort to equalize the chances. The staking of
equal sums on a fair trial of speed and endurance was the
simplest way for noblemen to indulge their gambling instincts
with horses.

Of course, it did not take long for others to join in the fun.
They soon discovered that one did not need to be an owner
to bet on the horses; that such wagering could be a pleasurable,
even profitable, pastime; and that vast numbers of all ranks felt
the same way. Thus the stake money contested by the owners
was invariably but a small fraction of the amount to change
hands over the result, and when two really good horses were
matched, the excitement engendered was intense, the betting
furious.

For two centuries – the formative period of the thoroughbred horse – the match race was the most common method for
testing the species. Fortunes were won and lost, reputations
built and shattered, and the very progress of the breed made
dependent upon this sudden death, winner-take-all basis.
It clearly had its drawbacks, and by the mid-nineteenth century
the practice was dwindling, stifled by the realization that bigger
fields produced truer results, less frequently distorted by the
tactics of the men on top.

Yet when match races were about to die their natural death,
the greatest of them all took place at York, on May 13 1851.
This was the year when the Great Exhibition was getting all

7

the Londoners excited; when an American called Singer produced a new-fangled gadget which did your sewing for you; and when a double-decker omnibus first appeared on the streets.

These were all mighty fine ideas, of course, but to a Yorkshireman they could hardly compare with the scene on the Knavesmire, York's own racecourse, when Voltigeur accepted a second challenge from The Flying Dutchman – two winners of the Derby and St Leger, both trained in Yorkshire, battling out a power struggle over a testing two-mile circuit. This was a match made almost by public demand, so much controversy having surrounded their previous meeting at Doncaster in the previous Autumn. The nominal stake was but £1000 a side, Lord Zetland against Lord Eglinton. But the sums dependent on the outcome surely ran into millions.

The reputations of the combatants were phenomenally high. The Flying Dutchman had almost completed three seasons in training without a defeat when he went to Doncaster in September 1850, and it was not only fervent partisans who dubbed him 'Horse of the Century'. Then Voltigeur beat him and had a faultless record of his own. What can you call a horse who beats the 'Horse of the Century'?

The Flying Dutchman had been foaled in Co. Durham on February 27 1846, a son of Bay Middleton (himself an unbeaten winner of the 2000 Guineas and Derby) and Barbelle, a mare whose foal of 1844, Van Tromp, won the St Leger in Lord Eglinton's colours. The successes of Van Tromp encouraged the 35-year-old Scottish peer to pay 1000 guineas for the half-brother as a yearling, and it was an investment he was never to rue.

Brilliantly fast as a two-year-old, The Flying Dutchman won each of his five races, including the July Stakes at Newmarket and the Champagne Stakes at Doncaster. His trainer, John Fobert, did not bring him out at three until the Derby, which he won narrowly after being in some difficulty because of the excessively soft terrain. He followed by walking over for two minor events at Liverpool, then easily added the St Leger to his impressive list of credits.

To underline the fact that he had stamina as well as speed, The Flying Dutchman began his third season by landing the Emperor of Russia's Plate (as the Ascot Gold Cup was then known) by eight lengths over two and a half miles, beating the classic mare Canezou into third place, then had ten lengths to spare over the good colt Vatican in a Goodwood event over three miles five furlongs. It seemed that nothing could beat The Flying Dutchman, whose next objective was named as the Doncaster Cup. Everyone took it for granted that the 'Horse of the Century' would be permitted to walk over for his final success before being retired to stud.

However, Lord Zetland and his trainer Bobby Hill thought otherwise. With Voltigeur they had an unbeaten three-year-old who had several points in his favour. This 1000-guinea purchase by Voltaire had won his only race as a two-year-old in good style at Richmond; had scored an easy victory in the Derby despite the fact that his trainer had chosen the week before Epsom for a monumental drinking bout and left the colt unattended in a railway van for two days; and forty-eight hours before the Doncaster Cup had defeated Russborough in the St Leger, proving clearly the stronger in the run-off after first dead-heating. Moreover, it was common knowledge that The Flying Dutchman had not been trained seriously, in the belief that nothing would oppose him in the Cup. An unfit 'Dutchman' would really have to be a world-beater to outlast a tuned-up Voltigeur over two and a half miles, especially as the younger colt received an allowance of 19lb. Adding to the factors in Voltigeur's favour was The Flying Dutchman's jockey, Charles Marlow, and his fondness for a tipple. Charlie decided to celebrate his assured victory in advance, and was anything but sober when the mounting bell was sounded.

None of these elements could disturb the general impression that this was to be The Flying Dutchman's glorious finale, and he was heavily backed at odds of 1–4, while Voltigeur had few supporters outside the band of loyalists from Richmond, where he was trained.

Either through arrogance or drunkenness, Marlow totally ignored his orders, which were to set a slow pace for a mile and a half, then accelerate. Instead, he set off at a furious gallop and at one time held a lead of ten lengths. If he had been kept in strong work during the preceding weeks, The Flying Dutchman might have lasted home, but halfway up the final straight Marlow found that he had asked too much of his mount. Voltigeur caught him comfortably and jockey Nat Flatman pushed the younger colt out to a gallant half-length victory.

Doncaster had never known a race like it. The locals were ecstatic, for while both contenders were trained in Yorkshire,

9

the winner was owned by a Yorkshire peer whose popularity knew no bounds. But the arguments raged, as they were bound to do in the circumstances. Now everybody seemed to know that neither The Flying Dutchman nor his jockey had been in a condition to give of his best. The only resolution to the question must be a match.

Lords Eglinton and Zetland could not readily be made to agree to the proposal, particularly the former, who declared that he had already sold four-fifths of the shares in The Flying Dutchman, who was to stand at the Rawcliffe Stud in the following Spring. But public opinion was such that in November an agreement was reached in principle and a month later the York racecourse executive was able to announce that they would stage the contest over two miles for £1000 a side. The weights had still to be settled, and these were left to Captain (later Admiral) Henry Rous, who decreed that The Flying Dutchman should concede $8\frac{1}{2}$ lb to his younger rival.

Having set matters in train, the York executive were now made to realize what they had started. The interest aroused over the ensuing months was astonishing. The horses seemed so well matched that the betting was almost always 'evens each of two' and all manner of gossip and speculation surrounded the forthcoming event. As the great day drew nearer, the race committee appreciated what was going to happen.

The introduction of the railways had brought York closer to London, making an afternoon on the Knavesmire a perfectly feasible outing for those who insisted on taking their breakfast and dinner in town. There would also be Northcountrymen in their droves, riding, walking, or driving to the 'Match of the Century'.

A desperate appeal was accordingly delivered to York Corporation, begging for adequate police to control the throng, coupled with an offer to cancel the race in the event of an insufficient supply of officers being available. Happily, the Corporation was wise to the benefits of the tourist trade, and though it had not had to cope with such a vast influx of humanity since the public hanging of Eugene Aram 100 years before, it was able to guarantee the presence of half the county constabulary.

In fact the mob caused little trouble, although there were thousands present who failed to find a vantage point from which to witness any of the day's six events. The great attraction was the third race on the programme, following a couple of insignificant contests which just served to heighten the inevitable tension. Neither of the competing riders, again Flatman and Marlow, would take the risk of an injury in one of these earlier events, but this time neither took refuge from the occasion in the gin bottle.

As the pair cantered to the post, The Flying Dutchman's condition was universally admired. Hard and fit, bright in his coat, he showed all the power and symmetry which epitomise the top-class thoroughbred. Voltigeur, on the other hand, did not satisfy the critics by the way he covered the heavy ground, and there were those who found fault with his trainer for producing him so light. At the time of life when most horses gain weight and strength, Voltigeur had been worked to such a degree that he was now lighter than in his three-year-old days.

The tactics were different this time, with Flatman setting a sensible pace on Voltigeur, while Marlow sat still, observing his rival's every move from about three lengths away. Both jockeys rode confidently, Flatman intent on gradually quickening the speed to shake off The Flying Dutchman, while Marlow endeavoured to keep enough in reserve for a decisive final challenge.

The first indication of the eventual outcome came at the turn into the straight, where The Flying Dutchman edged closer to the leader without apparent expenditure of effort. But it was still too early for Lord Eglinton's dark brown five-year-old to make his bid for immortality. A short, sharp burst would provide the surest means of settling the younger colt's pretensions if he were not in prime condition.

The cat and mouse tactics were pursued until just over a furlong from the finish. Then the cheers reached a deafening pitch as perhaps the tenth of the throng who could see it heralded The Flying Dutchman's challenge and the other nine-tenths expressed their second-hand excitement.

'The Dutchman's coming!' 'Come on Charlie!' 'Volti's not beat yet!' 'Ride him Nat!' 'Wave that whip!' 'Drive him out!' 'Now you've got him!' 'Come on boyyyy!'

It was one of those glorious sporting moments when enthusiasm borders on pandemonium, when the sheer thrill of the occasion communicates itself as vividly to the blind as to the sighted.

For an instant or two it seemed that Voltigeur might yet hold the Dutchman at bay. He answered Flatman's calls gamely, thrust his head down, and strove valiantly to maintain his advantage.

But The Flying Dutchman's remorseless stride was not to be denied now. His effort had been timed to a nicety. As the post drew near he, and only he, had the vital impetus, that powerful dark frame taking Marlow's flailing whip and pounding out more pace by way of answer.

Victory was his now and with every step the triumph became more complete – a head, a neck, half a length, until Judge Clark proclaimed his verdict. 'The Flying Dutchman by a length!'

Both horses bore the evidence of a struggle, decorated by scars from whip and spur. If Voltigeur seemed less so, it was only because Flatman had dropped his whip in the heat of the battle. Horses and spectators alike were drained of energy, the physical exhaustion of the former matched by the emotional prostration of the latter.

Understandably, Lord Eglinton announced The Flying Dutchman's retirement from the Turf immediately after the race. Incredibly, Lord Zetland elected to run Voltigeur again on the following day and his languid champion slumped to what was surely a predictable second defeat.

Voltigeur, indeed, was never the same horse again, but he retained enough of his vitality to make a significant contribution to the breed when he was retired to stud. Fittingly, he and The Flying Dutchman united to produce a future champion. Twenty years after their great struggle on the Knavesmire, Voltigeur's son Vedette was mated with The Flying Dutchman's daughter Flying Duchess, and the result was Galopin, hero of the 1875 Derby and an outstanding sire.

A MATCH. At York, Tuesday, 13 May 1851. Two miles. £1000 a side.

Lord Eglinton's br.h. The Flying Dutchman. 5yrs, 8st 8½lb
C. Marlow 1
Lord Zetland's br.c. Voltigeur. 4yrs, 8st 0lb   E. Flatman 2

    Winner bred by H. Vansittart. Trained by J. Fobert.

Betting: even.

Won by a length.

GLADIATEUR

*when the first great French champion completed a success
sequence unmatched before or since*

Researchers into the origins of the thoroughbred horse are divided as to how to interpret and attribute its excellence. The facts have long been lost in the passage of time, so those who credit the seventeenth and eighteenth century importations of Arabian, Barb, and Turkish stallions for adding refinement and stamina to the native strain may with equal safety be countered by those who argue that the indigenous English mares instilled the all-vital pace which became its most distinguishing feature.

But one statement will brook no contention. The thoroughbred is English. Here, without a shadow of a doubt, he was first bred, developed, and trained, and his supremacy established. To this day all thoroughbreds born in France are officially designated *Pur Sang Anglais*. The correct term for German thoroughbreds is *Englische Vollblutpferde*. And so it is, around the globe. Only the Americans, still smarting mentally over 1776 and all that, seem to have forgotten.

The English are fortunate to be identified by the French and Germans with the most elegant and noble species on Earth, while we think of them in terms of champagne and sausages. However, while the best champagne remains French and the best sausages are invariably German, the best thoroughbreds are now only sometimes English.

By the start of the eighteenth century it had been proved beyond doubt that no Arab horses could match the thoroughbred (the *English* thoroughbred) under racing conditions. We began to export fine specimens of our new breed, plus some of the expertise which developed, trained, and rode it. But our arrogance passed unchallenged when we attempted to stage races in which foreign-bred horses were permitted allowances of weight. The English were best, and the foreigners knew it too.

Such pride, and its attendant complacency, invited a fall.

It took a long time, but when it came it was complete. The first gentle blows were inflicted by the German colt Turnus in the 1850 Stewards' Cup and by the French filly Jouvence in the Goodwood Cup three years later. A deeper scar appeared in 1864, when the first foreign victory in an English classic race had to be recorded. That was the Oaks, won by Fille de l'Air.

Worse was to come, for within a couple of years the myth of England's invincibility on the Turf had been demolished by a series of hammer blows that resounded throughout the racing world. The 2000 Guineas, the Derby, the Grand Prix de Paris, the St Leger, the French St Leger, the Ascot Gold Cup – no horse, before or since, ever compiled such a sequence as the mighty Gladiateur. And Gladiateur was French.

A son of the prominent French stallion Monarque, out of a crippled mare called Miss Gladiator, this colt had raced three times as a two-year-old, winning on the first occasion in good style. He then ran third, after suffering bad luck in running, for a competitive Prendergast Stakes and retired for the season following a complete failure in the Criterion Stakes. The reason for his starting in the last-named race was best known to his trainer, for it was common knowledge beforehand that the colt had been coughing and had temporarily lost his form. He was not even quoted in the betting and he finished nowhere.

Gladiateur's juvenile form was that of a potential top-class colt, but there were several who were rated more highly as the 2000 Guineas of 1865 drew nearer. He started at 7–1 for that classic, only fifth in the betting, on account of the common belief that he was no more than half-fit. Such was probably the case, but a half-fit Gladiateur was too good for fully wound-up rivals, and he got home by a neck after a close struggle with Archimedes and Liddington.

The writing was clearly on the wall now for England's chief Derby hopes, and a week before the Epsom meeting a correspondent in *The Sporting Times* was moved to forecast victory for Gladiateur with the doom-laden words, 'Waterloo will be avenged'.

Sure enough, fifty years to the month after Bonaparte could finish no nearer than third to Wellington and Blücher on the Belgian plains, the son of one of his generals, Comte Frédéric de Lagrange, reversed the form on Epsom Downs. Gladiateur, the angular bay colt he had bred at his stud in Normandy, streaked home three lengths ahead to capture the so-called 'Blue Riband of the Turf'.

The battle analogy quickly took the public fancy, with the result that Gladiateur is known to this day as 'The Avenger of Waterloo'. And the massive bronze statue which greets visitors to the paddock at Longchamp remains to preserve the memory of the day when French racing achieved parity with English.

His Derby performance proved Gladiateur to be a great horse, and all England loves great horses, whether home- or foreign-bred. Yet it was not the destiny of Monarque's son to become one of those champions that the public takes to its heart, cherishes, and idolises. His defects of conformation (his forelegs were said to be atrocious) could have been forgiven; his 'Frenchness' was excusable; but the unpopularity of Lagrange and his trainer, Tom Jennings, knew no bounds. Their ever-dubious, often downright dishonest conduct made few friends.

The general enmity towards 'the French stable', as Phantom Cottage in Newmarket was invariably known, was based on no isolated instance of sour grapes from a jingoistic home contingent. There were so many concrete examples of trickery to be laid against them – notably the pulling of horses, running to deceive the handicapper, and manipulation of the betting market. Even its best horses were not immune from this shabby and shameful treatment, with the result that Press and public alike were alienated.

The Press, far less restrained in those days, openly called Lagrange a crook. They dealt Tom Jennings (an Englishman, incidentally) similar heartfelt abuse. The public had no doubts that the pair were villains and there were several ugly scenes on racecourses when retribution was demanded and very nearly exacted by a furious mob. A couple of instances must suffice.

When Fille de l'Air landed a great gamble for the stable in the 1864 Oaks, having previously cost the public a fortune by her inexplicably bad running in the 2000 Guineas, the angry Epsom crowd sought out Arthur Edwards (the filly's rider in both races) and intended to give him a hiding. They failed only because the leaders of the revolt mistook his colours for those worn by Harry Custance, who only just explained his identity in time. Meanwhile, Edwards and Fille de l'Air were speedily guided back to the weighing room by three mounted policemen and half a dozen professional pugilists, the famous Jem Mace included.

Fifteen years later, Jennings ran two horses in the Rosebery Stakes at Epsom – Paul's Cray in his own colours and Phénix in those of Lagrange. Phénix was the obvious form horse, and the public backed him freely at odds of 4–6. But the stable's money was piled on Paul's Cray at the last minute at all rates down to 3–1, while the favourite's price drifted to 2–1. The public knew they had been robbed before the race started, but the manner of its confirmation incensed them to violence which was, if not justifiable, at least understandable. When Paul's Cray took the lead, Phénix's rider, Jem Goater, simply watched him go, making not the slightest effort to chase. Only the police saved Goater and Jennings that day, yet the Jockey Club Stewards held that the miscreants had no case to answer!

Such were the deeds of Lagrange and Jennings, the talented but twisted connections of Gladiateur. No wonder that the average racegoer did not share the unbridled joy at the successes heaped on Phantom Cottage.

It was undoubtedly the stable's record of low cunning and open deceit which gave birth to the scandalous rumour that Gladiateur was a year older than his birth certificate claimed. It was never, it *could* never be substantiated, but the mud was slung and some of it stuck simply because people could believe the French stable capable of anything.

During his two-year-old days, Gladiateur was more than once described as 'looking like a three-year-old'. There was nothing sinister in that, but by the following Spring *The Sporting Times* was alluding to how 'conveniently' Gladiateur's dam had aborted her foal of 1861. The obvious inference was that Gladiateur had been foaled in that year and had spent two seasons in the yearling paddocks. It had been done before and just *might* have happened again in this case. If it had, it was common knowledge that an ordinary four-year-old could beat a classic three-year-old at level weights, so Gladiateur was no great shakes.

The rumours were current throughout the summer, as Gladiateur picked up the Grand Prix de Paris in easy fashion, came home by 40 lengths in one race at Goodwood, and was allowed to walk over for another. The affair came to a head two days before the St Leger, when William Graham, a gin distiller who owned the Oaks winner Regalia, petitioned the Doncaster Stewards to ban Gladiateur from running in the classic unless the colt was first examined by veterinary surgeons and proved to be a three-year-old.

The Stewards declined to entertain Graham's plea, asserting that he had produced no good reason for doubting the colt's eligibility. Perhaps that was true, but a simple examination of Gladiateur's teeth – all that would have been necessary – could have cleared so many doubts. The officials were doubtless embarrassed by the position in which Graham placed them and they were motivated primarily by the thought that the slightest hint of scandal would threaten the newly acquired respectable image of Doncaster races.

So it was that Gladiateur ran, won effortlessly, and Regalia finished second to him. To mark his gratitude to the town of Doncaster, Lagrange made the munificent gesture of donating to local causes – £50 to the Infirmary and £25 to the Catholic Church!

By the end of the season there was no doubting Gladiateur's predominance over the three-year-old generation, but the doubts persisted as to whether he should rank among them or above them. Happily, the chance came to make a proper assessment, for the French colt was kept in training for a third season.

If he were really a five year-old in 1866, his superiority over those who raced against him as contemporaries in the previous year would surely be less marked. It is a proven fact that horses develop appreciably from three to four years, but the rate of progress (if there is any at all) is checked thereafter.

Thus, when the Ascot Gold Cup came along, there was more than passing interest in how Gladiateur would shape against Regalia, who had been three lengths behind him in the St Leger. There was also another, and many felt more important, factor, which concerned Gladiateur's fitness for the gruelling two and a half miles of the Cup course.

From the time when he came into training, Gladiateur had suffered recurrent bouts of lameness. Some called it navicular disease, others blamed bad joints. Whatever the cause, Gladiateur was frequently lame and the condition deteriorated as he got older, providing Jennings with a load of problems. Just before Ascot, the Newmarket wiseacres (who always know best until the facts invariably prove them wrong) insisted that the colt should be at even money for the Gold Cup – evens he won, evens he broke down!

When the race got under way, there was reason to believe

that the touts might be right for once, as the three runners passed the stands with a circuit to race. Breadalbane, the outsider, set a strong gallop, closely pursued by Regalia, while Gladiateur lay well back in the rear. The fact that Harry Grimshaw, rider of the champion, was notoriously short-sighted did little to reassure supporters of the favourite as Breadalbane sped happily away, with Regalia keeping him close company.

The margin between the first two and the favourite continued to widen until by halfway, with a mile and a quarter to run, Gladiateur was at least 300 yards in arrears. Had those 'dicky' legs failed him at last? Had Grimshaw taken leave of his senses? Could his eyesight be *that* bad? Surely no horse, however brilliant, could make up that amount of ground in so short a time?

The bookmakers could not conceal their delight at the apparent certain defeat of the favourite. They would have loved Breadalbane, almost friendless in the betting at 20–1, to maintain his lead, but Regalia would do almost as nicely, for all the 'swells' had plunged on Gladiateur at 2–5.

Lagrange, though, had no doubts. It was at this point that Admiral Rous turned to him to say that surely Gladiateur had no chance from that position.

'Mais, monsieur l'amiral, c'est absolument certain', replied Lagrange, who undoubtedly knew his horse. Almost as he spoke, the deficit started to diminish. Breadalbane was coming to the end of his tether, while Regalia was not progressing with much fluency.

Meanwhile Grimshaw edged closer, and before the entry to the straight, even allowing for his deficient sight, he must have had the leaders in view. In fact he soon lost sight of Breadalbane again, for that colt dropped right back, completely exhausted by his pacemaking efforts, and Harry Custance was obliged to pull him up before the post was reached.

When well round the final turn, Gladiateur drew up to Regalia. A minute before a loud-hailer could not have produced a conversation between the jockeys. Now Tom Chaloner glanced to his left, found the massive bay colt about to smother his mount for speed and gasped, "You've done me, Harry.'

Grimshaw barely had time for the briefest 'Good-bye' as Gladiateur's never-faltering strides pounded him clear of his rival. The crowd erupted and the cheers reached a deafening crescendo as the favourite's margin extended with every bound. It had hardly seemed possible that so much ground could be yielded and retrieved. Now it was being converted into a massive advantage.

When he arrived at the post, Gladiateur had 40 lengths to spare, and now it was Chaloner who had difficulty keeping Grimshaw in sight. Never had there been such a transformation in a prestige race, never such overwhelming domination.

A vast throng hailed the champion as never before. Some had always doubted his pedigree. Others had queried the merits of the rivals he had conquered. Still more had withheld their enthusiasm because of their antipathy towards his connections. Now they gave a great horse his due, cheered him to the echo, lauded him to the skies. There was no disputing his quality after this. The thoroughbred had reached another pinnacle in its development, and what did it matter if the French had produced him?

Gladiateur ran only once more, recording an easy victory in the Grand Prix de l'Empereur at Longchamp. He then retired to stud, but died at the age of 14 without having sired a single worthy performer. The proud epithet 'Avenger of Waterloo' was his and his alone.

GOLD CUP. At Ascot, Thursday, 31 May 1866. Two and a half miles. £650 to the winner. For 3-year-olds and up.

Comte F. de Lagrange's b.c. Gladiateur. 4yrs, 8st 10lb
                                              H. Grimshaw 1
W. Graham's ch.f. Regalia. 4yrs, 8st 7lb   T. Chaloner 2
H. Chaplin's ch.c. Breadalbane, 4yrs, 8st 10lb H. Custance 0

Winner bred by Comte F. de Lagrange. Trained by T. Jennings.

Betting: 2–5 Gladiateur, 3–1 Regalia, 20–1 Breadalbane .

Won by 40 lengths; Breadalbane was pulled up. Time 4min 35.5sec.

ORMONDE

*when the leadership of an outstanding generation was
settled in sensational style*

April 25 1886 brought one of those bright but chilly mornings
for which Newmarket Heath has been renowned for centuries.
Keep on the move and it's a beautiful day; stand or sit idly
around and you can feel the cold germs infiltrate your system.

On the morning in question the vast, open spaces of the
Bury Side gallops were comparatively deserted; it was a
Sunday and many Victorian trainers would not dream of
exercising their horses on the Lord's day. There were, though,
some 20 horses at work, directed by men no less God-fearing
than their fellows but more mindful that when their charges
needed exercise they must have it, Sunday or no.

Over yonder, sitting astride his cob, was Mathew Dawson,
doyen of the training fraternity. A formidable character in every
respect, this 66-year-old Scot had achieved almost everything
a trainer could strive for – four wins in the 2000 Guineas,
three in the 1000 Guineas, four in the Derby, four in the Oaks,
and five in the St Leger. Indeed, he felt that he had done
enough and had planned to retire at the end of 1885. The
scheme looked likely to materialise when he quit his beloved
Heath House in Newmarket at the beginning of October, but
he got no further than Exning, a couple of miles down the
road, where a few special friends persuaded him to carry on
training a reduced string for his remaining years.

There was one good reason why the dour Mat, normally an
obstinate creature when his mind was made up, had given way
to that pressure – Minting. In 1884 Dawson had had the good
fortune to train St Simon, whom he and many others regarded
as the finest racehorse who ever trod the Turf; in 1885
Minting's performances as a two-year-old suggested that
lightning had truly struck twice in the same place. He was
surely a potential world-beater and the prospect of saddling
him for the highest honours in 1886 was exactly the spur the
old gentleman needed.

And there was the little white-haired genius, his eagle eye scrutinizing every movement as each horse passed him, making mental notes of their condition and measuring, to a nicety, their improvement. That Minting. What symmetry! What physique! What action! How he would show them all the way home in the 2000 Guineas on Wednesday.

Meanwhile, in the distance, the only other trainer on the Bury Side that morning was putting a few through their paces. He did not really belong there at all, for he was John Porter, a 48-year-old downsman from Kingsclere, on the Hampshire-Berkshire borders. He had started as a stable boy, progressed to being a rather unsuccessful jockey, then rapidly to the peak of the training profession. He had saddled nearly 500 winners in some 20 seasons, including three of the Derby, two of the 2000 Guineas, and one each of the 1000 Guineas, Oaks and St Leger.

Porter was a long way from home, but he was here for an excellent reason – supervising a small raiding party for the Newmarket First Spring meeting, due to be held from Tuesday to Friday that week. Most especially he was here to saddle Ormonde, his unbeaten champion, for the 2000 Guineas on Wednesday.

These were two proud men who hailed each other from afar that fresh spring morning. These were artists, fine craftsmen who had laboured long years in the pursuit of perfection. Now they were both confident that they had achieved it. The public unveiling would be next Wednesday, on the time-honoured Rowley Mile, but a private showing for a respected fellow artist was surely appropriate now.

In the rough Scots burr which half a century spent south of the border had failed to change, Dawson called to the lad in charge of Minting to bring the colt over for Porter's inspection.

'I'm aboot to show ye the best horse ye've ever seen in your lafe, John', the old man croaked, making no attempt to conceal his pride but consciously trying to overawe his younger colleague.

The pair sat motionless for a minute or more as four of the most practised eyes in racing sized up this magnificent specimen – strong, powerful, handsome, standing on the best of legs. He had to be admired from every aspect.

Of course, the best-looking horses are often poor runners. But there was exceptional merit in that big frame too. As a two-year-old he had raced five times, winning the Seaton Delaval Stakes at Newcastle, the Prince of Wales's Stakes at Goodwood, the Champagne Stakes at Doncaster, the Triennial Produce Stakes and Middle Park Plate at Newmarket. His record was faultless. And his breeding left no room for doubt – by the Triple Crown winner Lord Lyon out of Mint Sauce. Here was speed and stamina in an ideal blend.

Porter could only express his genuine admiration for Minting and the condition Dawson had wrought on him, but he found no reason to feel put out by the old man's confidence.

'Now how about a look at my candidate, Mat? Bring Ormonde for Mr Dawson to see,' he called enthusiastically, and a grand, imposing bay stepped out of the ranks to be paraded for inspection.

Here was the colt who had made his début in the race before Minting's Middle Park victory last October. That was only a minor event, but he had won well against a filly called Modwena who had already won eight of her ten races. After that Ormonde had cantered away with the Criterion Stakes by three lengths and the Dewhurst Plate by four lengths, making some of the fastest youngsters in training look like cripples.

Dawson was bound to confess that he liked Ormonde. He liked the colt's breeding too – by Derby winner Bend Or out of the Ebor Handicap winner Lily Agnes – but on conformation points he could not really compare the colt with Minting. Overall, Minting was much the finer physical specimen, and when it came to racing, Dawson even had a vision of how Wednesday's race would develop.

'Ye will hear them shouting Ormonde and Saraband home much of the way, but when they get into the Dip it will be "Minting" and nothing else. My horse will leave them all there, John, ye'll see', vowed the old man, utterly convinced that his representative was about to prove himself the eighth wonder of the world.

Porter, to his credit, would not be outgunned in this psychological battle, countering with an almost insolent. 'Don't be too confident, Mat. In all probability it will be in the Dip that Minting will get left behind.'

Neither trainer had his confidence shaken by this brief encounter on the gallops. But each was profoundly impressed by the condition of the other's contestant, and each knew well that the winner would have to be the greatest 2000 Guineas winner of all time.

There was a third colt who could enter the argument and show that this was no two-horse race. His name was Saraband, an elegant chesnut colt by Muncaster out of Highland Fling who had won six of his eight races as a two-year-old. His only defeats came at Kempton Park, when he failed by a short head to give 13lb to a smart filly called Sunrise, and in the Middle Park Plate, when he went under by a neck and a head to Minting and Braw Lass.

Saraband had to be taken seriously, for the most brilliant jockey of the time, Fred Archer, was to ride him. He had ridden Ormonde to all his victories, and Minting to three of his, but Saraband claimed his allegiance for the 2000 Guineas. No doubt the vast retainer given him by the colt's owner, John Blundell Maple (later Sir John, MP for Camberwell and a noted philanthropist), had some influence on Archer, but winners were always more important than money to him and he would not have accepted the mount if he felt he had no chance of success.

When the six runners – the other three seemed forlorn hopes – arrived at the post, Minting was a heavily backed favourite at 11–10, with Saraband at 3–1 and Ormonde only third best at 7–2.

The start was somewhat farcical in that Viney, who rode 200–1 shot Coracle, tried to steal a march on the others, much to the annoyance of the starter, Lord Marcus Beresford. Coracle, like Ormonde, was owned by the Duke of Westminster, and Porter started this colt with the intention of ensuring a true gallop for the stable's chief hope. After being repeatedly called back to line up with the others, Viney exclaimed to Lord Marcus, 'What's the use of me coming down there when I have to make running for Ormonde?' The starter's verbal retort to that stunning logic has not been preserved, but we do know that he insisted on Coracle starting with the other five.

In fact the start was the only moment when Coracle stood on even terms with the rest, for he was caught flat-footed when the flag fell and never looked remotely like fulfilling his pacemaking role. The Westminster colours, though, were to the fore throughout, for George Barrett had Ormonde swiftly away, closely attended by Minting, on whom Jack Watts was clearly intent to chase and then pounce.

By the end of the first furlong Ormonde and Minting were out on their own and already it seemed that this was a trial of strength which concerned just these two massive bays. Way behind, Saraband was cutting no sort of figure.

The pace stepped up, Ormonde's great devouring strides matched constantly by Minting's, while the other four runners struggled and abandoned all hope. It was as though the pair were staging an exhibition gallop, dictating the terms, showing why the phrase 'poetry in motion' is so appropriate to the thoroughbred at full stretch.

Barrett and Watts rode like demons. After all, they had been so instilled with confidence by their respective employers that they had nothing to fear. Each believed that there was no limit to the capabilities of his mount, so each pulled out all the stops in the carefree anticipation that victory was assured.

However, when races are run from end to end, with two jockeys intent on cutting each other down, one horse invariably cracks. There cannot be two winners (except in very exceptional cases) and more often than not in these circumstances the winning margin is not very close. With no chance to get his second wind, the horse who yields first is generally beaten easily.

So it was here, for although the two were almost stride for stride as they came to the descent into the Dip, the writing was already on the wall for one of them. Ormonde galloped relentlessly, inexorably on, but Minting was plainly coming to the end of his road. The change of gradient, after being under constant pressure for six and a half furlongs, flattened Minting's effort. He rolled. He swayed. He 'changed his legs'. Watts strove hard to gather the colt together, but his impetus had gone beyond recall and all the jockey could do now was to push him out with hands and heels, keep him on a straight course, and maintain a respectable second place.

Ormonde was on his own now, two lengths clear and looking as though he was enjoying himself in an exercise gallop on those rolling downs at Kingsclere. Only this was no half-speed work with stable companions; this was a duel between champions, at racing pace throughout the finest mile race in history. And Ormonde was the king.

There were still two lengths between the principals at the finish, but nobody bothered to assess the margin between Minting and the third, Mephisto, who was simply described as 'a bad third'. Saraband came in a disappointing fourth.

The defeat of Minting was a shattering blow to Mathew Dawson, who had never given a thought to such an eventuality. He promptly withdrew from public gaze for the rest of the week, reiterating the words 'Minting's beat' until finally convinced that his eyes had really told him the truth. When at last he came to terms with the facts, Dawson abandoned the classic route he had planned for Minting and diverted him to Longchamp for the Grand Prix de Paris, which he won very easily by two lengths to underline the class of his 2000 Guineas conqueror.

Indeed, Ormonde never lacked reflected glory from the achievements of his victims, and if he virtually settled the championship of the 1886 classic campaign on his first outing of the year, that was by no means the summit of his career. There were twelve more outings and no defeats, so that his final record read 14 wins and 2 walks-over from 16 starts over three years.

In the Derby he scored one of the easiest victories on record over The Bard, who had raced unbeaten through 16 outings as a two-year-old and was rated good enough to have won nine out of ten Derbys. The Bard suffered only one other defeat in his life – when trying to concede 31lb to Riversdale in the Manchester Cup – and there can be no doubt that his form entitled him to be regarded as a very high-class horse.

Perhaps the highest compliment ever paid to Ormonde was when he walked over for a private sweepstakes at Newmarket in October 1886, six weeks after he had completed his sweep of the Triple Crown in the Doncaster St Leger. In this mile and a quarter event, the weights were so arranged that Ormonde should carry the same as the previous year's Derby and St Leger winner Melton (trained by Mat Dawson) and should give The Bard an allowance of 10lb. Melton's owner, Lord Hastings, and The Bard's owner, Robert Peck, paid a forfeit of £500 each rather than risk having their champions humiliated by the Duke of Westminster's wonder horse. On those terms, they should both have beaten him, but everybody knew that Ormonde was far more than a Derby winner, far more than an exceptionally good Derby winner. He was the best there had ever been.

Ormonde's career from the St Leger onwards was hampered by the scourge of roaring, a wind infirmity which finishes most horses for racing purposes. The vets could not cure it and John Porter related how the ailment became so bad that on one foggy morning at Kingsclere the horse could be heard breathing nearly half a mile away.

Even in that condition, Ormonde showed prodigious ability as a four-year-old. He gave the subsequent St Leger winner Kilwarlin 25lb and beat him by six lengths in the Rous Memorial Stakes; overcame foul riding tactics from an opponent and just got up to beat his old rival Minting in the Hardwicke Stakes; then took on the high-class sprinter Whitefriar at his own game, conceded 6lb and beat him easily by a couple of lengths in the Imperial Gold Cup over six furlongs.

Those were the performances of a horse sorely afflicted in his breathing; they would rate the adjectives 'exceptional', 'outstanding' or 'impressive' from any horse in the pink of condition. It is awesome to contemplate what deeds a fully fit Ormonde might have accomplished.

Ormonde held undisputed sway over the most talented generation in racing history, yet he is generally compared unfavourably with St Simon, two years his senior, when discussion turns to the greatest horse of the nineteenth century. St Simon never ran in a classic race, nor did he beat any thoroughly top-class horses when they were at their peak; the assumption of his superiority to Ormonde on the racecourse is a myth based on two false premises.

The deeds of a horse's offspring always lend colour and lustre to the parent, so that St Simon has figured ever more largely in people's thoughts. He was one of the most important stallions of all time, whereas Ormonde led a miserable stud existence in England, the USA, and Argentina and proved almost infertile.

Fred Archer has been frequently quoted as saying that St Simon was the better racehorse and, as he rode them both, his word is regarded as law. However, it should be pointed out that he rode St Simon only as a two-year-old and thus was not equipped to compare the two when they were at the height of their powers. The great jockey was dead within a few days of Ormonde's last victory as a three-year-old, so it would be interesting to know when the alleged statement was made.

A likely explanation is that Archer did not express that view at all. It seems odd that almost the only person who could remember the comparison being made was the Duke of Portland, who just happened to own St Simon. It is a fact that

26

when Archer was interviewed in America in December 1884, he told the Press:

'There was nothing very wonderful about the three-year-olds (in England this year), but St Simon, I imagine, is about the best, and St Gatien a good one and very improved of late.' That was after St Simon had retired and the champion jockey evidently had no great opinion of the colt's merit then.

That quote, coupled with Mat Dawson's fervent belief that Minting would prove the best horse anyone had ever seen, influence me to think that Ormonde established his right to the 'Horse of the Century' title when he reduced the trainer of St Simon and Minting to incoherence and amazement with his victory on the Rowley Mile. Confirmation came at Ascot a year later in the only other defeat Minting ever suffered – again by Ormonde, truly a giant among giants.

2000 GUINEAS. At Newmarket, Wednesday, 28 April 1886. One mile. £4000 to the winner. For 3-year-olds only.

Duke of Westminster's b.c. Ormonde. 9st 0lb	G. Barrett	1
R. C. Vyner's b.c. Minting. 9st 0lb	J. Watts	2
Prince Soltykoff's ch.c. Mephisto. 9st 0lb	T. Cannon	3
J. B. Maple's ch.c. Saraband. 9st 0lb	F. Archer	4
Duchess of Montrose's br.c. St Mirin. 9st 0lb	F. Barrett	5
Duke of Westminster's bl.c. Coracle. 9st 0lb	A. Viney	6

Winner bred by Duke of Westminster. Trained by J. Porter.

Betting: 11–10 Minting, 3–1 Saraband, 7–2 Ormonde, 100–3 St Mirin, Mephisto, 200–1 Coracle.

Won by 2 lengths, a bad third. Time: 1min 46.6sec.

PERSIMMON

when the nation's best-loved son, Prince Teddy, won the nation's most glittering prize

There was much that did not amuse Queen Victoria, and racing came high on her list of pet hates. She was taken to see her first Derby in 1831, when she was only 12 years old, but the occasion did not inspire her. A few years later it behoved her to attend Ascot, but she felt only bored indifference to the racing and total anathema for the gambling.

Within six months of her accession to the Throne, the Hampton Court Stud, developed so promisingly by her uncle, William IV, was disbanded, the stock being sold at auction in October 1837 for a total of 15,692 guineas. The thought of having horses in training herself would never have crossed her mind and not until 1851 was she persuaded by her beloved consort, Prince Albert, that the re-institution of the Royal Stud would be both acceptable and responsible. Having acceded to the request, Victoria took not the slightest interest in its affairs, with the result that the stud, situated in Bushey Paddocks at Hampton Court, suffered the most appalling mismanagement and met with almost no success for a quarter of a century. The tide turned with the arrival of Springfield (foaled in 1873) and later came classic winners like Sainfoin (Derby), Memoir (Oaks, St Leger) and La Flèche (1000 Guineas, Oaks, St Leger).

However, by the time of those later successes in the early 1890s, Victoria's eldest son, Albert Edward, was an important figure in the racing and breeding world in his own account. He first registered his colours as an owner in 1875, when he became a keen supporter of steeplechasing, and in 1886 he branched out into flat racing and founded his own Sandringham Stud.

The old lady disapproved from the start. She had always felt that Teddy spent too much time leading the social set and advertising his irresponsibility for affairs of state. Indulgence in racing was just one more wasteful leisure activity, and an indiscretion which was ever in the public eye. But Victoria could check it no more than she could check the Prince's many other social follies and dalliances, which were to delight his biographers in later years.

Racing had Prince Teddy hooked, and he was not ashamed to admit that he enjoyed every aspect of it, betting included. Unlike his mother, the general public doted on him the more for it. His frequent visits to the racecourse testified further to his evident enjoyment of life; his preference for a degree of informality brought him the welcome image of 'a man of his people'. The populace saw in Teddy the prospect of a brighter era for a Britain struggling to cope with the manifold problems of an increasingly industrial society. The man and woman in the street were able to identify with Teddy, something which was impossible with the ageing widow of Windsor, whose old-fashioned aloofness could inspire no more than a distant devotion.

Teddy made a happy choice when he selected John Porter as his first flat race trainer and professional adviser. The Kingsclere maestro not only set the Prince on a sound footing as an owner; he provided his Royal patron with the basis for unimagined success as a breeder by purchasing Perdita as one of the foundation mares for the Sandringham Stud. For an outlay of £900, this mare by Hampton benefited the Prince's exchequer by some £250,000, as her offspring won £72,913 in stakes, three of them earned about £150,000 in stud fees, and one was sold abroad for 30,000 guineas.

Unfortunately for Porter, the vast majority of that income accrued after HRH had removed his horses in training from Kingsclere and placed them in the care of Dick Marsh at Newmarket. This incident has never been properly explained – Newmarket was certainly far more convenient to Sandringham, but there was more to it than that. It may be that Porter and the Prince's racing manager, Lord Marcus Beresford, failed to concur on some aspect of the running of the Royal horses; HRH himself was always ready to acknowledge his indebtedness to the master of Kingsclere.

Florizel, by St Simon out of Perdita, was the first notable winner Marsh saddled for the Prince. This colt, whose victories included the St James's Palace Stakes, the Manchester Cup, the Ascot Gold Vase, the Goodwood Cup and the Jockey Club Cup, was at his peak in 1895, when his younger brother was just beginning to make a name for himself.

That name was Persimmon (a grandiloquent version of date-palm) and he showed Marsh early in his two-year-old career that he was easily the pick of the stable's youngsters. His racecourse début was set for the Coventry Stakes at Royal Ascot and he did not disappoint, storming home three lengths clear of some useful rivals. Following an impressive gallop at level weights with the excellent three-year-old sprinter Ugly, Persimmon started an odds-on favourite for the Richmond Stakes at Goodwood and came back a comfortable winner by a length. Ugly, a son of Minting, made the form look better by landing the Singleton Plate two days later.

Persimmon's only subsequent race that year was the Middle Park Plate, in which he ran contrary to the wishes of his trainer, for he had been coughing for fully two weeks before the event. Lord Marcus Beresford insisted that the colt should run and he even started favourite, but lack of condition told against him and he went down by half a length and four lengths to St Frusquin and Omladina. Jack Watts was not too severe on him when victory became an impossibility, but that was the solitary redeeming feature of a result which seemed to indicate that St Frusquin had the 1896 classics already in his pocket.

There was no reason to amend that impression in the early Spring, when Persimmon's home gallops were so bad that Marsh was forced to withdraw him from the 2000 Guineas. St Frusquin, who had already won the Column Produce Stakes at the Craven meeting, won that classic as well with ridiculous ease. The filly Thaïs gave Prince Teddy and his trainer some consolation by scoring a well-merited win in the 1000 Guineas, but it was hard to forget the fact that the stable's Derby hope still failed to thrive.

Marsh now determined that only work, work, and more work would get the thick-winded Persimmon into shape for Epsom. Improvement came steadily in response to this rigorous programme, so that three weeks before the classic Marsh felt confident enough to invite Lord Marcus Beresford down to witness a full scale Derby trial. The trainer was certain that he now had Persimmon in a condition to reveal his true ability at last, but instead the colt trailed a moderate animal called Safety Pin by four lengths and Marsh's face was redder than ever. 'A nice sort of Derby horse', was Lord Marcus's sarcastic observation as he left to contemplate the débacle on his way back to London.

However, that poor effort was not repeated in the ensuing weeks' work, from which Marsh could only derive the utmost satisfaction with the colt's condition, willingness, and apparent ability. The only anxiety the colt caused now came at the eleventh hour, when he steadfastly refused to enter the railway box which was to take him to Epsom. Two trains left Dullingham Station, his boarding point, without him and with no more than a quarter of an hour remaining before the departure of the last available train, there was still no indication that Persimmon would have a change of heart.

Marsh was beginning to think that his long months of dutiful devotion to this highly-strung individual were to be wasted. The kindness and understanding he had lavished on Persimmon were being rewarded with pig-headed non-compliance. It was too much for the trainer, who risked his own sanity and injury to the horse by calling for volunteers to bundle the cussed brute into the van. Happily, Persimmon finally consented to be lifted bodily aboard and he gave no more trouble on the journey.

Derby Day was sultry, the going was hard, and the crowd was of almost record proportions. Nobody had much doubt that St Frusquin would win and he was a firm favourite at 8-13. But inwardly almost everybody hoped that a miracle would occur and Persimmon could bring victory to the nation's favourite, Prince Teddy.

Persimmon, who had sweated up at Goodwood as a two-year-old, broke out freely while being saddled at Sherwood's stable near the start. The fact that he did not have to be subjected to the parade (it was optional in those days) was doubtless in his favour, for the bustle and frenzied activity, added to the thinness of the air, would have drained him of the nervous energy he needed for the struggle.

The eleven runners got away well after four or five false starts, with the outsiders Toussaint and Bradwardine foremost. Bay Ronald, later to become an influential sire, took over before a furlong was completed, setting a respectable gallop while Tommy Loates, on St Frusquin, and Jack Watts, aboard Persimmon, sat calmly in the rear, concerned more with each other than how things were up front. Gulistan, a stable companion of St Frusquin, was the next to take a turn in the lead, but it was only on sufferance. By the time they reached the top of the hill, half-way through their journey, St Frusquin had moved up smoothly into third position and Persimmon was making steady headway in pursuit.

Before rounding Tattenham Corner, St Frusquin had only Bay Ronald in front of him, while Persimmon moved into third place and was poised to challenge. The odds-on chance now seemed likely to justify the confidence of his backers, but there remained a possibility that the Royal colours could yet come to the fore.

With over a quarter of a mile to run, Bay Ronald dropped out, leaving St Frusquin in front and Persimmon as the only conceivable danger. Remarkably, the normally silk-smooth action of the Rothschild colt was not developing the pace everyone had anticipated. There had been talk that he was a chronic sufferer from rheumatism; you could believe that now as Persimmon, who had not been on a racecourse for nearly eight months, drew up to him and was surely going the better.

The effect of this revelation on the crowd was electric. The favourite was going to be beaten, but almost every one of the quarter million or so spectators could not care less. Prince Teddy was going to win the Derby!

St Frusquin clearly could not shake off Persimmon now. The first cheers rang out prematurely a furlong from the finish, as Watts sat calmly half a length behind his rival, but going significantly the stronger of the pair. It was obvious from the stands that the Royal colt could go past at any time his jockey chose.

Watts, with iron nerve, elected to delay that moment until the final hundred yards and when it came it was as though the colt's momentum sprang from the wave of tumultuous cheers which broke out.

Driving his mount rhythmically now, Watts urged Persimmon's head in front and Loates was powerless to retaliate. As the post drew nearer, Persimmon edged ever so slightly further away and you could have called the neck margin cheeky as the multitude erupted in delight.

A mighty roar arose as the number '1' was hoisted into the frame. Peers and plebs alike were unrestrained in their enthusiasm. Silk hats and flat caps were consigned to the air in careless rapture. It was the most frenetic display of communal delirium racing has ever inspired.

All eyes turned towards the Club Stand, from whose balcony the Prince had watched the contest. At first he was content to stand there and acknowledge the acclamation from that safe perch, but the scene so impressed him that he felt bound to descend to the lawn, to mingle with his loyal subjects, and to lead his champion back to scale. The risk to life and limb was considerable, but it was a gesture Teddy owed to this vast throng who loved him and were so delighted to share in his hour of glory.

The cheers were renewed as Teddy took Persimmon's rein and led him through a mass of back-slapping patriots to the weighing room door. If HRH had ever doubted his popularity, he never would again. An hour or so later, his day was complete when a telegram of congratulation arrived from Balmoral. The Derby she saw 65 years before may not have amused the Queen, but she appreciated what the winning of it meant. Teddy was to relive the experience twice more, with Diamond Jubilee in 1900 and Minoru in 1909, but the felicity of that first success could never be matched.

There was a sense of anti-climax about Persimmon's next appearance, for he was beaten, but it was a most honourable defeat by half a length against St Frusquin (who was receiving 3lb) in the Princess of Wales's Stakes at Newmarket. Thereafter it was triumph all the way, with victories in the St Leger and the Jockey Club Stakes to close 1896 and stunning performances in the 1897 Eclipse Stakes and Ascot Gold Cup to wind up his racecourse career. As a stallion he found immediate fame as the sire of Sceptre, who remains the only outright winner of four English classics, and he was champion sire four times although he died at the early age of fifteen.

DERBY STAKES. At Epsom, Wednesday, 3 June 1896. 1½ miles. £5450 to the winner. For 3-year-olds only.

HRH Prince of Wales's b.c. Persimmon. 9st 0lb   J. Watts   1
L. de Rothschild's br.c. St Frusquin. 9st 0lb   T. Loates   2
H. E. Beddington's br.c. Earwig. 9st 0lb   F. Allsopp   3
B. S. Straus's br.c. Teufel. 9st 0lb   F. Pratt   4
L. Brassey's b.c. Bay Ronald. 9st 0lb   W. Bradford   5
L. de Rothschild's b.c. Gulistan. 9st 0lb   T. J. Calder   6
A. Calvert's br.c. Bradwardine. 9st 0lb   F. Rickaby   7
J. Wallace's b.c. Spook. 9st 0lb   R. W. Colling   8

H. McCalmont's br.c. Knight of the Thistle. 9st 0lb

                                     M. Cannon 9

E. Cassel's b.c. Toussaint. 9st 0lb   J. Woodburn 10

L. Brassey's b.c. Tamarind. 9st 0lb   H. Grimshaw 11

Winner bred by HRH Prince of Wales. Trained by R. Marsh.

Betting: 8–13 St Frusquin, 5–1 Persimmon, 100–9 Teufel, 25–1 Bay Ronald, Knight of the Thistle, 33–1 Gulistan, Earwig, 40–1 Bradwardine, 100–1 Spook, Toussaint, 1000–1 Tamarind.

Won by a neck, 4 lengths. Time: 2 min 42 sec.

ABOYEUR

when the King's horse killed a suffragette and the stewards
disqualified the winner

The Derby of 1913 was not only the most sensational classic ever run at Epsom; it is doubtful whether there has ever been a horse race to match it for excitement, intrigue, and tragedy. Some of the odder aspects remain unexplained to this day. On consideration of the facts, as they were presented at the time, it would appear that only the Stewards behaved fairly throughout. In retrospect, reading between the lines here and there, one wonders whether any of the actors in this dramatic episode should emerge with credit. It was a thoroughly unsavoury business from beginning to end.

Epsom was clear and bright on that first Wednesday in June – the perfect setting for what had long been regarded as every Londoner's annual day out. Absenteeism was passively, if not actively, encouraged – if the boss could go to the races, so could the workers. There was always such a mass of humanity at Epsom that the odds against being spotted were astronomical.

This year the throng had a sound choice to back in the year's greatest race – Craganour, easily the top two-year-old of 1912 and the recent comfortable winner of the Newmarket Stakes. The odds against him were short – only 6–4 – but he seemed a certain winner and any price about a certain winner was something for nothing. No wonder the hundreds of thousands descending on Epsom Downs by train, motor car, foot, and omnibus were so light-hearted. What a day this was to be! What a day, indeed.

There was one person who alighted from her train at Epsom that day with something else on her mind. This was a serious young red-headed woman from Morpeth, Northumberland, intent on one of the most sensational – and successful – publicity stunts of all time.

Emily Wilding Davison was a militant suffragette who had tried all the recognised methods for advancing the cause she supported so vigorously. Between March 1909 and November 1912 she had served eight terms of imprisonment for offences like stone throwing, setting fire to pillar-boxes, and smashing windows in the House of Commons. The last sentence had been something of an embarrassment – ten days for assaulting a person she mistook for Lloyd George. In fact her victim was a Baptist minister.

This time she would erase the memory of that fiasco with a daring manoeuvre which would focus world attention on the Women's Social and Political Union. A gifted, inspirational writer with a Bachelor of Arts degree from London University, she found herself frustrated when editors declined to publish her letters to the Press.

Frustration turned to fury when five of her colleagues were imprisoned for attempting to present a petition to the King while he was on his way to open Parliament. That was a few weeks before the Derby, an occasion always attended by the King and Queen, and this year the King would himself have a runner – Anmer. As soon as Miss Davison learned that, her own personal petition to the King was conceived – a courageous, even reckless move, but a move virtually guaranteed to gain sympathy for the cause of women's suffrage.

She did not miss a trick in her planning. She chose Tattenham Corner, the most famous landmark on the course, as the scene for her demonstration. She familiarized herself with the purple and gold colours to be worn by the King's jockey. And, conscious of the dangers, she pinned two large green and white suffragette flags to the inside of her coat, ensuring that, whatever happened, everyone would know the reason for her action.

Her strategy prepared, Emily Davison positioned herself behind the inner rail at Tattenham Corner and waited, praying that Anmer would not be hidden from view by any of the other fourteen runners.

She need not have worried on that score, for Anmer was a distinctly modest performer and by the time he got to Tattenham Corner he was already almost tailed off. The leader, about three lengths' clear, was Aboyeur, chased by the hot favourite Craganour, with Day Comet, Shogun and Louvois next. Anmer came down the hill just to the rear of Agadir, with Nimbus alongside him and only two, Jameson and Sandburr, behind him.

The militant timed her death and glory run to perfection,

darting under the rail as Agadir, Anmer, and Nimbus approached. Deftly nipping by under Agadir's neck, causing a startled Walter Earl to snatch his mount up and swerve violently away, the tall redhead then calmly positioned herself directly in Anmer's path.

Herbert Jones, the Royal jockey, had no chance to take avoiding action – not that Miss Davison would have allowed it. She held out her arms, willing a collision, and tried desperately to grab the reins as the colt hit her head-on.

Jones was catapulted out of the saddle, but luckily clear of any further danger. Temporary concussion, abrasions to the face, and bruises all over his body were his uncomfortable but fortunate fate.

Miss Davison got the martyr's death she probably craved – crushed by half a ton of Anmer. Fracture of the skull and haemorrhage of the brain were the official causes of her death, which took place four days later in Epsom Cottage Hospital. While she lay there unconscious, the Queen sent for word of her condition; the King, it is said, enquired only after the health of his jockey, who recovered quickly in the same hospital. Perhaps that symbolized His Majesty's non-acceptance of even this desperate petition. The coroner at the inquest recorded that he did not think Miss Davison aimed at the King's horse in particular – an incredible conclusion to draw in the prevailing political circumstances and in the light of photographic and eye-witness reports.

One tragedy enacted, the scene was set for another drama with far-reaching consequences. Leaving Anmer to recover his feet and his composure, the other fourteen made their way home in varying degrees of tiredness caused by the strong early gallop.

With three furlongs to run, Aboyeur, having been in front from the start, seemed about to forfeit his advantage. The 100–1 shot had exceeded most people's expectations by leading thus far and as Craganour drew alongside, it appeared to be the favourite's race. But it was not as simple as that.

Shogun, the second favourite, made strong headway to reach a challenging position. By the two-furlong marker, when Aboyeur was fighting hard to retain his lead on the rails and Craganour kept going strongly on the outside, Shogun's rider Frank Wootton decided the time had come for his effort. He started to drive his mount towards the gap between Aboyeur and the rails – a gap which he later described as large enough to accommodate a carriage and pair – but in next to no time there was no gap at all.

Aboyeur was now hard by the rails and Wootton, obstructed, frustrated and in some danger of his life, screamed at Edwin Piper, the rider of Aboyeur, to 'for God's sake keep your horse straight'. Piper yelled back that it was not his fault, implying that Johnny Reiff, on Craganour, had driven him there.

Moments later, Wootton saw a second chance up the rails. Again he was shut off at the crucial moment, apparently by Craganour's edging across and squeezing Aboyeur towards the fence.

The finish, meanwhile, drew nearer, and with only 300 yards to race the favourite gained command, leading by half a length. Then, just as suddenly, he faltered and Aboyeur was level once more. Again Craganour claimed a narrow advantage; again Aboyeur fought back and this time it must have seemed to Reiff that the challenger was bringing reinforcements. Louvois and Day Comet had passed Shogun and were bearing down fast near the rails. Great Sport and Nimbus – the latter had been far enough back to see the suffragette incident, but had made tremendous headway in the straight – were generating their best pace up the stands side.

There was plenty of room for Louvois and Day Comet to deliver their efforts as Craganour and Aboyeur were by now at least 15 feet off the rails – photographs published later confirmed that fact. The reason for that was that Aboyeur had over-reacted to Piper's left-handed whipping, had veered sharply to the right, bumping Craganour and taking him wide. Great Sport and Nimbus had been making their challenges wide enough, but now they were carried even further to the outside as Piper either could not or would not change his whip hand. While only Aboyeur and Craganour actually touched, Great Sport and Nimbus were clearly affected.

They flashed past the post with Craganour a head in front of Aboyeur. Day Comet was a head away third, another head in front of Louvois. On the stands side, Great Sport came fifth, just over a length behind Louvois and a head in front of Nimbus. Shogun and Sun Yat were clearly seventh and eighth.

The judge, Charles Robinson, wasted little time in ordering the result to be posted. Up went No. 5 – victory for Craganour, the favourite, and the crowd went wild. Aboyeur was placed second, Louvois third and Great Sport fourth.

Robinson had bungled badly, completely failing to notice Day Comet's hearty late challenge up the far rails. There is not the slightest doubt that he was in the group of four who finished 'all of a heap'; there is excellent photographic evidence to prove that in fact he finished third.

It was easy to be wrong in a blanket finish like that, and Judge Robinson had none of the mechanical aids which his counterparts of later years have enjoyed. To err is human, but Robinson stretched his display of humanity too far here, with his second catastrophic blunder in a classic race in two months.

There was only one person who believed that Louvois had won the 2000 Guineas – Judge Robinson. Everyone else on the course *knew* who had won – Craganour. He had led by four lengths with two furlongs to race and had held on well, with speed to spare, although challenged hard by Louvois. Certainly Johnny Reiff conjured a powerful run from Louvois, but there was never a doubt that Craganour won. His jockey Bill Saxby, swore that the margin was half a length.

The Stewards then, the Hon. Frederick Lambton, Major Eustace Loder, and Lord Wolverton, saw no reason to question the judge's decision and the result was allowed to stand.

At least Craganour had now gained some consolation for that mistake, with victory in the greatest of all classics. His owner, Charles Bower Ismay, who had bought him as a yearling at Doncaster for 3200 guineas, led the colt proudly back to scale through the cheering, milling throng.

Of course, most people in the stands had seen the barging match which had occurred, but it was clearly a case of 'six of one and half a dozen of the other'. Piper declared, before he got to the weighing-room, that he had no reason to lodge an objection, so it appeared that all was well.

Within a couple of minutes, someone in the weighing-room area called out 'All right', and the red flag bearing those words was hoisted to signify that the result was confirmed. Bower Ismay proudly accepted the congratulations of his friends; Jack Robinson revelled in that supreme emotion known only to the trainer of the Derby winner.

It was all dreadfully short-lived. As Craganour was about to be led from the unsaddling enclosure, an official sent by the Stewards shouted to the colt's attendant, 'Come back'. After another two-minute delay which must have seemed like hours, the red 'All right' flag was hauled down; instead, the blue 'Objection' flag was raised.

At first it was hard to take this move seriously, and odds of 4–1 were laid against Aboyeur being declared the winner. But it soon became apparent that things were very serious indeed for the backers and connections of Craganour. The Stewards themselves had objected to the winner on a charge that he had jostled the second horse.

The Stewards were Major Eustace Loder, Lord Wolverton, and Lord Rosebery, but as the last-named had had a runner in the race – the filly Prue, who finished tenth – it was decided that he should not adjudicate on the objection. It was a strange concession to fair play in the circumstances.

It was mooted, and later admitted, that the prime mover in the decision to object was Eustace Loder, who just happened to be the breeder of Craganour. What makes a man want to disqualify a colt he has bred to win the world's greatest race? Duty? Fair-mindedness? Or hate?

The witnesses were called and Craganour's fate was sealed. Bill Saxby gave his evidence. The man who had ridden Craganour in the 2000 Guineas and had been replaced by Reiff in the Derby was hardly likely to say anything which would benefit the American jockey or the colt's connections.

The judge gave his evidence. The man who had already cost Craganour the 2000 Guineas and had just blatantly misread the Derby finish was credited as a fair and impartial witness. His view was taken as conclusive.

For the first time since 1789 the winner of an English classic was disqualified for causing interference. Aboyeur was declared the winner, Louvois promoted to second (not bad for a colt who in fact finished fourth) and Great Sport was placed third. There was still no place for poor Day Comet.

It seems likely that Loder pressed for a disqualification because of the last-furlong incident, when Aboyeur was undoubtedly the culprit. But that was a fact not easily established from any other than a head-on position and it must have been a pleasant surprise for him to learn that there was evidence of other 'crimes' further down the course with which to charge Craganour.

Incredibly, having lodged the objection on a single charge of jostling Aboyeur, the Stewards eventually disqualified him on the twin grounds that 'Craganour, by not keeping a straight course, had at one point in the race seriously interfered with

Shogun, Day Comet and Aboyeur, and had afterwards bumped and bored Aboyeur so as to prevent his winning'.

It is possible that there was some merit in the first reason, but the second was outrageous. A head-on camera patrol film, something which Stewards had to do without for another 50 years, would have shown conclusively that it was Aboyeur's abrupt swerve from the rails which caused the collision and seriously inconvenienced both Great Sport and Nimbus. Photographs published later showed just how far Aboyeur had drifted across the course by the finish, at which time Piper still had his whip in his left hand and his mount was still leaning on Craganour.

Craganour was fated not to win because his own breeder did not want him to win and had acted as both prosecution counsel and judge at the enquiry. Loder received a lot of harsh criticism for his action and it was stated openly that his reason was a personal grudge against Bower Ismay.

The allegation is not as far-fetched as it might seem. Ismay was the son of the founder of the White Star Line, and he had himself been a passenger on the maiden voyage of its greatest creation, the *Titanic*. In the aftermath of that tragedy a lot of bitter insinuations were made, justly or unjustly, pointing to the 'interesting' detail of Ismay's survival on the night 1517 other passengers and crew were drowned. Whatever the facts about that episode, Bower Ismay did not acquire popularity as a result.

It was also asserted that Ismay was something less than open in his dealings on the Turf. Less than four months before the Derby he had had two winners in a week, at Birmingham and Hurst Park, both of whom showed remarkable improvement in form. The Stewards of the National Hunt Committee enquired into the alleged offences and withdrew the licence of Ismay's trainer, Tom Coulthwaite. The fact that Coulthwaite was not permitted to resume training until 1921 indicates that the 'crimes' were held to be of a very serious nature. No action was taken against Ismay, but the public undoubtedly held him to be at least partly responsible and as far as racing's rulers were concerned, he was thereafter a 'marked man'.

Eustace Loder had sold Craganour privately as a foal to the Sledmere Stud, whence Ismay had bought him at public auction. The connection between owner and breeder seems tenuous enough, but it is not difficult to imagine that any involvement would rankle with Loder, a Steward of the Jockey Club who had always conducted his racing affairs with impeccable propriety and sportsmanship. By disqualifying Craganour and depriving Ismay of victory, he endeavoured to create right by committing a second wrong.

Loder justified his action with noble words, querying whether his critics would prefer a Steward to shirk his duty and ignore palpable infringements of the Rules of Racing. Nevertheless, the disqualification of Craganour preyed on his mind for the remaining 13 months of his life, which ended after a lingering and extremely painful attack of Bright's disease. A fulsome obituary referred to him as a man 'whose every thought and action was inspired by kindness and charity'.

Ismay, a cynical fellow at the best of times, accepted the verdict with quite good grace, knowing well the reason for it. He even gave his trainer and the stable staff the presents he had earmarked for them in case of victory. But he could not bear the thought of racing Craganour again, and three days after the Derby the colt was sold to the Argentine breeder Miguel Martinez de Hoz for £30,000. He proved a great success as a sire in South America.

Aboyeur, who grabbed the glory, the £6450 first prize and an estimated £40,000 in bets for his connections, raced twice more and was beaten on each occasion. He was then sold for only £13,000 to the Imperial Racing Club of St Petersburg. Years later a romantic story was circulated to the effect that he and the 1909 Derby winner Minoru had been evacuated to Serbia during the Bolshevik Revolution. Two Derby winners harnessed together on a 1000-mile trek! It was one of those tales which, if it was not true, ought to have been.

Thus ended perhaps the murkiest episode British racing ever staged. But it's an ill wind that blows nobody any good, and within a few years women had the vote. Whereas the names of Aboyeur and Craganour are almost forgotten, that of Emily Wilding Davison survives, representing a landmark in English social history.

DERBY STAKES. At Epsom, Wednesday, 4 June 1913. 1½ miles. £6450 to the winner. For 3-year-olds only.

A. P. Cunliffe's b.c. Aboyeur. 9st 0lb	E. Piper	1
W. Raphael's b.c. Louvois. 9st 0lb	W. Saxby	2
W. Hall Walker's b.c. Great Sport. 9st 0lb	G. Stern	3
L. de Rothschild's ch.c. Day Comet. 9st 0lb	A. Whalley	4
A. Aumont's ch.c. Nimbus. 9st 0lb	M. Henry	5
E. Hulton's ch.c. Shogun. 9st 0lb	F. Wootton	6
J. B. Joel's ch.c. Sun Yat. 9st 0lb	W. Huxley	7
Sir W. Nelson's ch.c. Bachelor's Wedding. 9st 0lb	S. Donoghue	8
P. Broome's b.c. Aldegond. 9st 0lb	G. Bellhouse	9
Lord Rosebery's ch.f. Prue. 8st 9lb	D. Maher	10
R. Bunsow's br.c. Agadir. 9st 0lb	W. Earl	11
Sir J. Willoughby's ch.c. Jameson. 9st 0lb	E. Wheatley	12
Mrs G. F. Rawlins's b.c. Sandburr. 9st 0lb	H. Jelliss	13
H.M. King George V's b.c. Anmer. 9st 0lb	H. Jones, brought down	
C. Bower Ismay's b.c. Craganour. 9st 0lb	J. Reiff, disqualified	

Winner bred by T. K. Laidlaw. Trained by T. Lewis.

Betting: 6–4 Craganour, 6–1 Shogun, 10–1 Louvois, Nimbus, 100–9 Day Comet, 100–7 Prue, 20–1 Great Sport, 25–1 Aldegond, 33–1 Bachelor's Wedding, Sun Yat, 50–1 Anmer, 100–1 Aboyeur, Agadir, Sandburr, Jameson.

Winning margins given as a head between Craganour and Aboyeur, a neck between Aboyeur and Louvois. Great Sport officially named fourth, Day Comet, the actual third horse to finish, not placed by the judge.

Time: 2min 37.6sec.

PHAR LAP

when the New Zealand wonder horse put the Americans firmly in their place

The thoroughbred racehorse is easily the best documented species in the world today. Some 50 years before Englishmen were required by law to register the births of their children, the breeders of thoroughbreds were already dutifully recording the arrivals of foals and submitting details to Mr Weatherby, who edited and published the *General Stud Book*. The same gentleman collected and collated the information for the *Racing Calendar*, setting down the exploits of those same foals when they came to pursue the activity for which they were bred – racing.

Now we have no fewer than 37 volumes of the *General Stud Book* and there have been 200 annual editions of the *Racing Calendar*, plus the equivalent publications issued in every other thoroughbred racing country. Yet with all this accurate documentation the practical breeder is no nearer an answer to the question, 'How do I breed a good horse?' It is a simple matter to increase milk yield in a dairy herd, and to obtain more meat from beef cattle or sheep, but the science of genetics has never been applied in such a way as to aid the production of superior athletes. We continue to rely on trial and error; we are compelled to grasp at the solitary straw which suggests that if both parents are good, the chances of their offspring also being good are marginally better than if they were not. Or, as one noted breeder put it a long time ago, 'Breed the best to the best, and hope for the best!'

The maxim clearly has some merit, and the notion is fine for those who can afford it. But it bears no guarantee of success and the history of the thoroughbred abounds with examples of those who came into life apparently with nothing going for them, yet who showed the so-called aristocrats what racing was all about. Such a horse was Phar Lap, bred on no kind of principle at all, unless it was 'breed the worst to the worst'. He looked just what might have been expected, a coarse, ugly brute. But he proved himself the greatest race-horse of his era, and in Australasia his name is uttered with reverence to this day.

That eventuality seemed remote, to say the least, when the colt was conceived in November 1925. His sire, Night Raid, had the unenviable reputation of being the ugliest stallion in New Zealand. His racing record in England had been deplorable – he probably hit his nadir when well beaten under 6st 12lb in a selling nursery handicap at Warwick – and he was sold as a two-year-old for 120 guineas. His buyer was Ayr trainer John McGuigan, who passed him on to the Sydney trainer Peter Keith.

To give Night Raid some credit, he improved a shade in his new surroundings and managed to dead-heat for first place in a small event. Then he changed hands again 'for a few hundred' in the deal which took him to a stallion career at Seadown Stud in Timaru, in the northern part of New Zealand's South Island. Mr. A. F. Roberts owned the stud and the sire. He also owned the mare Entreaty, who had broken down after her one and only (unsuccessful) racecourse venture. From such unpromising material, Phar Lap was created.

When the Australian trainer Harry Telford thumbed through the catalogue for the 1928 Trentham Yearling Sales, his eye fell on lot 41, the Night Raid–Entreaty colt. Years ago, in his riding days, Telford had often partnered a good stayer called Prime Warden, whose dam was Miss Kate. That mare just happened to be the fourth dam of lot 41. Although he had never seen the youngster, the trainer was determined to have him. As all trainers must, he then had to use his powers of persuasion on a client, and he found a somewhat reluctant David Davis who said he would take the colt as long as the cost was no more than 200 guineas. Praying that that sum would be sufficient, Telford wrote to his brother Hugh in New Zealand and instructed him to buy the colt. He got him for only 160 guineas.

Harry Telford may or may not have been delighted by his first view of the big, unsightly colt when he arrived from Wellington. Having been so determined to get him, he had to show some sort of enthusiasm. But David Davis was thoroughly disenchanted with the horse's appearance and he began to regret his modest outlay. Accordingly, Telford quickly concluded a deal whereby he would lease the colt from Davis for a three-year period, undertaking to pay all expenses himself for two-thirds of any prize money won.

The ungainly colt was christened Phar Lap, the Sinhalese for 'lightning', but it was a long time before he gave any promise of living up to the name. The yearling's legs of steel and powerful rump encouraged Telford to believe that this was a top-class performer in the making, but he was too big and backward to train seriously at this stage. Therefore Phar Lap was gelded, turned out, and given time to develop before being subjected to the rigours of a proper preparation.

Phar Lap did not appear on a racecourse until February 23 1929, when he made no sort of show in a modest nursery handicap at Rosehill. Five weeks later he had a record of four races and four unplaced efforts – hardly a distinguished start to his career. However, on April 27, he won the Maiden Juvenile Handicap at Rosehill over six furlongs to conclude his first season on a more promising note.

In the Southern Hemisphere horses take their ages from August 1, so it was as a three-year-old that Phar Lap returned to racing on the third of that month. In fact, he had four outings during August, but failed to reach the first three on any of them. Eight times unplaced from his first nine starts did not read like the record of a future champion. Yet he was to finish unplaced only once more in his life.

The first public indication of Phar Lap's true merit came in the Chelmsford Stakes at Randwick on September 14. Here he took on a top-class four-year-old called Mollison and gave him a real fright, displaying his massive 25-foot stride in a powerful stretch run which brought him a well-merited second place.

The promise was fulfilled a week later in the Rosehill Guineas, when Phar Lap proved an easy winner and at once became a strong contender for the A.J.C. and Victoria Derbys. Telford was quite confident of victory in both classics, but he warned backers not to bet on the gelding for the Melbourne Cup.

'Even if he wins the Derbys in the easiest manner, he will not run at Flemington. He is still undeveloped and the Cup could prejudice his future,' said the lessee-trainer, knowing full well that David Davis, the gelding's actual owner, *had* backed Phar Lap for the historic handicap.

Phar Lap duly won both Derbys, and the Craven Plate in

between, in such a style that Telford could not resist a tilt at the Melbourne Cup. He was to regret his change of mind, for the gelding failed to settle properly, tried to slip his field six furlongs from the finish, but tired in the straight to finish only third. A three-month rest was then prescribed, which did Phar Lap the world of good. When he returned in February 1930 he really filled out that massive red frame, but he was not fit enough to do himself justice at the first time of asking, running third in the St George Stakes.

Now followed a sequence of nine magnificent wins, with Phar Lap displaying complete domination over other top-class rivals at all distances from nine to 18 furlongs. The Victoria and A.J.C. St Legers were among the triumphs, but the outstanding performance came in the A.J.C. Plate when he beat Nightmarch (his conqueror in the previous year's Melbourne Cup) by 10 lengths in record time for the two and a quarter miles. While he was winning that event, he also smashed the Australian records for 12, 13, 14, 15, and 16 furlongs. No wonder that he acquired the nickname 'Red Terror' and that owners of other good horses strove hard to avoid him.

Yet if Phar Lap's performances as a three-year-old stamped him as the overwhelming champion of his generation, how should one begin to describe his form as a four-year-old? He was beaten a short head in his first race and a neck in his last, but in the 14 intervening races he ran unbeaten, sweeping aside the best horses in training on weight-for-age and handicap terms, at distances ranging between seven furlongs (with 10st 3lb in the saddle) and two miles. In the Melbourne Cup he started at 8–11, the shortest priced favourite on record, and carried 9st 12lb to a comfortable victory. His burden was 9lb more than any four-year-old had previously carried when winning the Cup. Moreover, that was the sixth of eight successes gained in a phenomenal five-week period, testifying to the gelding's extraordinary soundness.

Phar Lap returned in similar sensational style as a five-year-old, opening with eight consecutive wins, five of them during October. That was a typically testing preparation for his third attempt at the Melbourne Cup, on November 3, but this time the handicapper quashed any chance he might have had by setting him to carry the monster burden of 10st 10lb. It was an astonishing compliment to be paid, but it was unrealistic to consider his winning. He finished eighth behind the winner White Nose, who was receiving no less than 3st 12lb from the champion!

After the 1931 Melbourne Cup, David Davis had issued a challenge via the world's Press. 'Phar Lap', he said, 'will race any horse any distance for any amount.' There had been no takers. That was not good enough for Davis, who was insistent that the world should know just how wonderful his horse was. He did not care where he had to go for the race and eventually he was quite happy to settle for Tanforan, Mexico, and the Agua Caliente Handicap, which offered prize money of $50,500. Phar Lap was already the record stakes-earner in Australasia and in the British Empire; victory in Mexico would bring him within striking range of the world record.

Phar Lap was now owned in half-shares by Davis and Telford, the trainer having been permitted to buy into the gelding for only £4000 on the termination of the lease arrangement. Davis decided to make the long trip with the horse and share in all the ballyhoo; Telford stayed at home with the rest of his string, quite content to leave Phar Lap's training to the man who knew him best of all, his devoted stable lad, Tom Woodcock.

Always a horse with superb temperament, Phar Lap took the 10,000-mile sea journey as though he had been doing it all his life. He sailed from Sydney to California, stopping over for three weeks in Wellington, where thousands of New Zealand admirers came for a glimpse of the 'local boy who made good'. During his stay in his native land, Phar Lap was stabled at Trentham, just 100 yards from the auction ring where Hugh Telford had bought him for 160 guineas.

Phar Lap arrived in California on January 15, over two months before the race, which was held just over the Mexican border. Within a few days the gelding was in work, but it was work of a curious description as far as Americans were concerned. There were no fast trials. No proper gallops. Instead, Tom Woodcock rode Phar Lap around the countryside, up and down hills, in the style of the cow rancher. The gelding had never clapped eyes on the type of starting gate that was to be used, but Woodcock declined the opportunity for practice. 'He'll come away O.K.', was all the trainer would say.

The locals did not know how to take this foreigner. Certainly this was a most impressive, powerful horse. But it was surely lunacy to bring him 10,000 miles to a strange climate, with strange food, strange water, and an altitude of 6000 feet above sea level, and then treat him like a riding pony! Woodcock never ceased to astonish, particularly when he gave Phar Lap his one serious piece of work – three furlongs in 35 seconds – a week before the race and finally an hour before the race, when he ordered jockey Urn Elliott into the saddle just to get the gelding accustomed to carrying the full weight in the hot Mexican sun!

There had been 55 entries for this, the third running of the Agua Caliente Handicap, but only eleven went to post. Phar Lap was the top weight with 9st 3lb, and he was set to concede between 9lb and 39lb to his opponents, who included Spanish Play (winner of the New Orleans Handicap eight days before), Dr Freeland (winner of the 1929 Preakness Stakes) and Reveille Boy (winner of the 1930 American Derby and a recent Caliente victor). There were 15,000 spectators on hand, including many film stars who had flown in from Hollywood, congesting the little local airport.

The Agua Caliente management evidently believed in giving their patrons value for money, as the big race was the thirteenth of 15 events on the programme. They staged a memorable performance for the gala occasion.

As Tom Woodcock had predicted, Phar Lap was smartly into his stride, but Urn Elliott was unable to gain complete control in the early stages. The result was that horse took rider for a tour of the outer rail and by the time the first two furlongs of the mile and a quarter had been covered, they were 50 yards behind the pack. There was never cause for alarm, however, for Phar Lap soon settled quietly, remaining at the back of the field, but moving easily within himself.

With half a mile to run, Phar Lap produced a tremendous burst of speed which carried him from last to first in a dozen of those giant strides which had pulverised them all back home. It was the brand of acceleration which only a truly top grade runner can produce and it drew a gasp of admiration from the stands.

But it was not all over yet. Along came Reveille Boy, challenging hard off the bend, with the effrontery to draw level with Phar Lap. Elliott was merely giving the champion a breather, so he was not the slightest bit perturbed, but he felt it might be necessary to use his whip in case Phar Lap considered he had done enough. That was it. One tap and he was gone, bounding clear with effortless ease. Elliott was pulling him up again before the finish, where he was two lengths clear of Reveille Boy, a horse of his own age who received 11lb.

The time was a remarkable 2 minutes 2.8 seconds, a record for the track on a day when the going was not particularly fast. None of the other races on the card was run in a time anywhere near a record. Bearing in mind that Phar Lap had taken a circuitous route and was being pulled up before the finish, it was not surprising that the public gave him a standing ovation.

When he returned to the unsaddling enclosure, the gelding was mobbed by a host of admirers, but it was noticeable that they could not bother him any more than his opponents in the race. Phar Lap stood calmly at rest, unflecked by lather, as police tried vainly to stem the tide of well-wishers, but his composure was finally unsettled by the garlanding ceremony, which seemed to frighten the five-year-old. Then he backed away and stamped a foot on a concrete step, causing an injury which would rule out the thought of any further racing in the immediate future.

The exceptional merit of Phar Lap's performance excited enormous interest in the American Press, while breeding pundits the world over scratched their heads and pondered how this gelding 'by nothing out of nothing' could have achieved such greatness. That greatness is not in doubt. Eddie 'Banana Nose' Arcaro, generally reckoned to have been the finest jockey America ever produced, rode a winner at Tanforan that day. He always insisted that Phar Lap was the greatest thoroughbred ever to race on the American continent.

Tragically, there was only the Agua Caliente Handicap by which to measure Phar Lap's class away from home. While tracks all over the USA were competing for the honour of staging the gelding's next race and David Davis was attempting to cope with the mountain of offers, fate intervened to end speculation for good and all. Phar Lap, of the rugged constitution, winner of 37 of his 51 races, munched some grass in a paddock which had been sprayed with insecticide, was stricken rapidly with acute enteritis and died within hours.

The horse's connections, particularly Tommy Woodcock, were inconsolable. Australia regarded the news as a national disaster. The world demanded to know whether there was more to the catastrophe than met the eye. In time most people came to accept the truth of the autopsy report, but for years afterwards the subject could cause strain in US–Australian relations. It is related that during World War II convivial gatherings of American and ANZAC servicemen in the Pacific more than once turned sour with the question, 'Tell me, Yank. Why did your people poison Phar Lap?'

They hadn't, of course. Not intentionally. But how ironic that a weak solution of arsenic intended to destroy insects should snuff out the mighty heart of Phar Lap! For therein lay the secret of the 'Red Terror'. On the dissecting table it was learned that his heart weighed no less than 14lb – half as much again as that of the normal thoroughbred.

It was a phenomenon which had been noticed before, this correlation between outstanding racing merit and the possession of an outsize heart. Perhaps, after all, we should forget about breeding from stock with racecourse ability and beg the geneticists to help us to produce them big-hearted.

AGUA CALIENTE HANDICAP. At Tanforan, Mexico, Sunday, 20 March 1932. 1¼ miles. $50,500 to the winner. For 3-year-olds and up.

D. J. Davis & H. R. Telford's ch.g. Phar Lap. 6yrs, 9st 3lb

W. Elliott 1

J. A. Best's b.h. Reveille Boy. 5yrs, 8st 6lb   R. Wholey 2
J. D. Mikel's b.g. Scimitar. 8yrs, 7st 2lb   G. Smith 3
S. H. Lee's b.g. Joe Flores. 3yrs, 6st 6lb   S. Coucci 4
Mount Royal Stables b.h. Marine. 6yrs, 8st 2lb   F. Mann 5
J. Toplitzky's b.h. Good and Hot. 5yrs, 7st 4lb   W. Moran 6
Mrs J. A. Parsons's b.g. Seth's Hope. 8yrs, 8st 0lb   C. Turk 7
Knebelkamp & Morris's b.c. Spanish Play. 4yrs, 8st 5lb

C. Landolt 8

B. Creech's ch.h. Dr Freeland. 6yrs, 8st 8lb L. Cunningham 9
Oak Tree Stable's b.c. Bahamas. 3yrs, 7st 1lb   J. Longden 10
Mrs W. T. Anderson's b.g. Cabezo. 3yrs, 7st 2lb A. Fischer 11

Winner bred by A. F. Roberts. Trained by T. Woodcock.

Betting: 6–4 Phar Lap, 3–1 Spanish Play, 13–2 Joe Flores and Cabezo (coupled), 72–10 Reveille Boy, 106–10 Bahamas, 148–10 Dr Freeland, 186–10 Marine, 282–10 Scimitar, 414–10 Seth's Hope, 596–10 Good and Hot.

Won by 2 lengths, 3 lengths. Time 2min 2.8sec.

PINZA

*when the first jockey knight at last won the Turf's
'Blue Riband'*

Regarded in the simplest terms, the Derby is just one of the 3500 races run each year on the Flat in Britain – another betting opportunity like the race before it and the race after it. Bend the law of averages ever so slightly and you would believe that a jockey in the top flight for long enough would be certain of winning it (or any other given race) at some time: his number *should* come up. But it does not work that way. The best mounts have a habit of eluding the best riders, so that the richest rewards, the glory, the immortality a Derby win conveys, can often by-pass the real riding heroes.

Did you ever hear of Elijah Wheatley, Billy Higgs, or Willie Lane? Each laboured all season to become champion jockey during the present century, but they committed the 'crime' of failing to win a Derby and they are forgotten. Remember Joe Marshall, Freddie Lane, and Tommy Lowrey? None was ever at or near the summit of his profession, but their names will ever strike a chord, for they made the record books during those two and a half minutes of a June afternoon when all the world turns its eyes towards Epsom.

The injustice is harsh indeed, but Lady Luck seems always to have acted this way where the Derby is concerned. Among the great Victorian jockeys, Jem Goater failed to score in 28 attempts, George Fordham, Tom Cannon, and Nat Flatman had only one success each from 22, 24, and 26 tries respectively, and John Osborne had no fewer than 38 mounts for one solitary win. In more recent times, Doug Smith (will he be remembered in 50 years' time?) had 25 Derby rides which yielded him nought, while Michael Beary, Eph Smith, and Sir Gordon Richards each had only one victory to show for 28 efforts.

Of the last-named trio, Beary had 14 losers before his winning turn, while Smith had to wait only until his sixth ride. But Richards, perhaps the finest jockey Britain ever produced, was dealt Lady Luck's cruellest hand – a record 27 consecutive losers during a period when he was a record 26 times champion jockey.

As early as the 1930s the racing Press was filling columns with the story of the supreme rider who seemed fated never to become united with the supreme horse. Few of his early mounts in the classic had the remotest chance of success, but after he became attached to Fred Darling's all-powerful Beckhampton stable, he was almost always guaranteed a likely, not to say lively, contender. None could produce that magic spark on the day that mattered.

In 1933 Richards had the mount on Manitoba, who started second favourite but ran unplaced behind Hyperion; in 1934 he had the fourth favourite Easton, who was beaten a length into second place by Windsor Lad; in 1936, as Darling had nothing of consequence to run, he had the leg up on the Aga Khan's first string, Taj Akbar, but this 6–1 second favourite became another runner-up, beaten three lengths by his own stable companion, the 100–8 Mahmoud.

It seemed that the champion's turn had finally arrived in 1938, when Richards had the ride on Pasch, the 2000 Guineas winner, who started a hot favourite at 9–4. But for a second time he had the mortification of losing to a stable-mate, for Bois Roussel, a 20–1 chance also handled by Fred Darling, swept by Pasch and Scottish Union in the straight to win by four lengths. Richards was no nearer than third on the favourite, but he got one place nearer in the following year when he partnered Fox Cub, who was thoroughly beaten by an outstanding colt in Blue Peter.

The transfer of the Derby from Epsom to Newmarket for the war years brought no better fortune. Richards had the choice between Tant Mieux and Pont l'Evêque in 1940 and could hardly have forsaken the former after beating the latter about 100 yards in his final trial. But in the classic it was Pont l'Eveque and Sam Wragg who won, with Tant Mieux only fourth.

In 1941 there were several good colts in the Beckhampton stable, but Richards was convinced that Mrs Macdonald-Buchanan's Owen Tudor represented the best prospect for Derby honours. Things did not go quite according to plan in the 2000 Guineas, but the champion refused to become disillusioned, maintaining steadfastly that Owen Tudor would prove to be the pick of the bunch on Derby Day. This time he was right, but when the son of Hyperion flashed by his stable companion Morogoro to land the premier classic by a length and a half, the rider was Billy Nevett. Richards had broken a leg a few weeks earlier at Salisbury and was out of action for the season.

1942 was a banner year for Richards, who returned to the saddle in brilliant form, winning four of the five classic races. However, the Derby eluded him again, for the King's excellent colt Big Game, easy winner of the 2000 Guineas, failed to last the journey and was beaten into fourth place. Not even a 4–6 favourite could change the little maestro's luck! Another exceptionally brilliant, but temperamental customer, Nasrullah, carried him into third place in 1943, the year in which Richards cracked Fred Archer's lifetime score of 2748 victories.

In the second post-war Derby, now back at Epsom, Richards partnered what most people regarded as the colt who was certain to end the incredible hoodoo at the twenty-second attempt. This was Tudor Minstrel, unbeaten and a candidate for 'Horse of the Century' awards after his victory in the 2000 Guineas, when he streaked home by eight lengths with a display of superiority as overwhelming as had ever been witnessed in a classic. He started at 4–7 for the Derby, with only the 28,000-guinea yearling purchase Sayajirao remotely fancied against him; he was at 13–2. Tudor Minstrel beat himself, refusing to settle down and fighting to take control of his rider from the start. Although he led at Tattenham Corner, he was a spent force soon afterwards and he trailed in fourth behind Pearl Diver.

Richards rode another non-stayer, The Cobbler, in 1948, but in the following year found himself aboard another favourite, the fourth he had ridden in the race. This was Royal Forest, trained by Noel Murless, who had taken over Beckhampton from Fred Darling. A son of Bois Roussel, he had stamina enough, but failed to find the necessary pace to get to grips with Nimbus, Amour Drake, and Swallow Tail, who figured in the three-way photo-finish which so enthralled the crowds.

The Richards Derby hopes for the next three years were pinned to Napoleon Bonaparte (28–1), Stokes (20–1) and Monarch More (25–1), whose starting prices truly reflected their chances. They served only to extend the depressing record to 27 failures and ensured that by the time opportunity number 28 came around, the jockey would be a venerable 49 years old, still very sprightly, but surely running rapidly out of time.

The realisation that Richards had once again failed to make the winner's enclosure dimmed the glories of Derby Day annually for hosts of enthusiasts all over the world. For Gordon was regarded universally as something more than a worthy competitor dogged by ill-luck; in many people's eyes he was the outstanding sporting personality of his era. Incredibly gifted, invariably fair, disarmingly modest, he inspired affection like no other sportsman – one might almost say no other public figure – for over a generation.

His riding career spanned the period between Steve Donoghue's peak and the arrival of Lester Piggott. Throughout what has come to be recognised as the golden age of jockeyship in Britain – Michael Beary, Harry Wragg, Freddy Fox, Charlie Elliott, Rae Johnstone, Charlie Smirke, Tommy Weston, Billy Nevett, Brownie Carslake, Joe Childs, Eph Smith, Bobby Jones, Doug Smith, Harry Carr – Richards was ever the master. A world record number of winners, a total of 269 in 1947 which may never be beaten, a reputation unsurpassed in Turf annals. But never a winner of the Derby.

Then Pinza came into Richards's life, in a manner as surprising as it was sensational. Shortly before the 1952 Doncaster St Leger meeting, the Newmarket trainer Norman Bertie (former head man to Fred Darling at Beckhampton) asked the champion to come to headquarters to ride some two-year-olds in morning gallops. In particular, he wanted Richards to exercise Fountain, a contender for the Champagne Stakes who had shown plenty of promise when second to a fine filly called Bebe Grande in his previous race.

The batch was sent out to cover six furlongs with the order to keep the pace on all the way. If Fountain were a potential Champagne Stakes winner, he could be expected to pull away from his rivals at any point from halfway. If he drew away without much effort, he could be a classic hero in the making.

Richards soon found out that Fountain was no world-beater, for they had gone no more than a furlong when a big, burly bay colt, with George Younger in the saddle, pulled his way past to take the lead. From there on, Fountain's rider had only a diminishing sight of those vast bay quarters and the hitherto unknown colt finished the gallop the best part of a furlong in front of the supposed big race hope.

If Fountain had been known to be moderate, or had seemed unfit, the gallop might not have meant a thing. But the colt had good form to his credit and was clearly in excellent heart. That meant that the winner must be out of the ordinary, and Richards was quick to enquire who was this massive colt with the relentless, ground-devouring strides. Only then did Gordon become acquainted with Pinza, the horse who was destined to put paid to that seemingly endless Derby nightmare.

In fact, Gordon had ridden against Pinza little more than a month before, when Bertie gave him his introduction to racing in a small event, the Greensleeves Stakes, at Hurst Park. But the backward Pinza who could do no better than fifth in that modest company was unrecognizable from the obvious embryo champion who streaked clear of Fountain. Gordon would never want to oppose Pinza again, and he never did.

Fountain was comprehensively beaten by Bebe Grande in the Champagne Stakes, but was comfortably second best, so that Pinza must have seemed a gilt-edged investment in the next day's Tattersall Sale Stakes. So it proved, for he cantered home by six lengths to establish himself among the leaders of his generation.

Then, to advertise the truth of the old adage that nothing can make a fool of a man like a horse, Pinza contrived to be easily beaten by the Aga Khan's filly Neemah in the Royal Lodge Stakes at Ascot a fortnight later. Richards put the failure down to the colt's comparative lack of experience, and urged that he be given one more run that season. Bertie complied, allowing Pinza the chance to redeem his reputation in the Dewhurst Stakes, often the race which decides the juvenile championship. Now Pinza's class was evident for all to see, as he strode majestically clear of eight rivals up the final hill to win by five lengths.

Pinza was officially rated the third best colt of the season and went into winter quarters as many people's idea of the 1953 Derby winner. On his breeding, there seemed little doubt that he would be able to stay the Epsom mile and a half, and the public, almost to a man, wanted to believe what read like a fairy-tale – that Gordon would at last win the Derby, and on a horse bred by his old guv'nor Fred Darling and owned by another popular but very unfortunate sportsman, Sir Victor Sassoon.

Long before the new season arrived that dream had receded, thanks to Pinza's own natural high spirits. Always headstrong and self-willed, he resisted restraint once too often during the winter and slipped up on a road, damaging a shoulder. The injury held up his preparation for some time, then flared up again after it had seemed healed. Apparently a small piece of flint had remained in the wound and caused the recurrence.

In time, though, Pinza showed that his constitution was as tough as befitted a powerful, masculine, deep-bodied individual. By March, Bertie decided that the colt could be taken to Hurst Park for a gallop after racing, which would determine whether he might be trained for the 2000 Guineas. The spin, one mile over the round course with his contemporary Marche Militaire and the older Tobias, indicated that Pinza might yet be a classic horse, despite his winter misfortune – but that that classic would not be the 2000 Guineas. To hurry his preparation now would be prejudicial to his future. Patience was essential. Happily that was a quality which owner, trainer, and jockey knew well how to exercise.

The race selected for Pinza's reappearance was the New-market Stakes, an event since discontinued but formerly regarded as a useful stepping stone between the 2000 Guineas and the Derby over the intermediate distance of ten furlongs. An inspection of the colt in the paddock for that race did not instil confidence. He seemed too big and backward to acquit himself well, while Polynesian, who had won easily at Sandown Park, was a natural favourite at 7–4. Pinza was quoted at 3–1 here and at 33–1 for the Derby, still 24 days away.

The Newmarket Stakes did not go according to most pre-conceived notions. Pinza lobbed along in second place for seven furlongs, then strode effortlessly into the lead and raced clear of his five opponents. Richards was pulling him up well before the finish, which he reached with four lengths in hand over Polynesian.

Bookmakers at once reduced Pinza's Derby price to 8–1, though many of the professional element were not so keen to accept the form at face value. The opposition, they pointed out, had been negligible, while Pinza would find Epsom's undulating course a very different proposition from the straight ten furlongs at Newmarket. The critics called him coarse, heavy-topped, loaded in the shoulder and pointed to a pair of forelegs which, to say the least, would not normally be associated with a top-class horse.

Without a doubt Pinza had plenty of conformation faults which made him less than beautiful and raised doubts as to how long he would remain functional; these factors had to be weighed against his extraordinary strength and obvious ability.

By the end of that week the public had a second hero to fancy, for the Lingfield Derby Trial was won in exemplary style by the flashy chesnut Aureole, racing in the colours of the young and beautiful Queen whose coronation was due four days before the Derby itself. Richards knew well enough how impressive Aureole was, for he rode Prince Canarina into third place, beaten 11 lengths from the winner. He also knew – he had just been informed privately by Sir Winston Churchill – that the Queen had conferred the honour of a knighthood upon him. Despite the public's fancy for Premonition, a stable companion of Aureole, Richards knew that the royal colt was his only real danger – he would have to beat him to win the Derby. What a way to express one's gratitude for a knighthood!

When Derby Day dawned, Britain was basking in a state of euphoria unknown since VE Day. Within the last month, another of its sporting heroes, Stanley Matthews, had finally achieved his lifetime's ambition of an FA Cup winner's medal; the Commonwealth rejoiced in the conquest of Everest by Hillary and Tenzing; and, most recent of all, the splendour of the coronation united the free world in a spirit of friendship and jollity. These were halcyon days of sheer escapism; and the troubles of the world were ignored, if not forgotten. Now could it be that this tidal wave of euphoria would also engulf the Derby? Would Gordon at last reap his long-deserved reward, as Matthews had done at Wembley? Or would Her Majesty complete a right royal week with a classic victory to add to the ceremony in the Abbey? Many regretted that the interests of the two did not coincide.

With a vast Saturday crowd in holiday mood, fine weather, and perfect going, Epsom had everything that day. It even had two great racehorses. Pinza dominated his rivals in the paddock by dint of sheer strength and size. He looked somewhat less burly than at Newmarket three and a half weeks before, but again had a lad in the saddle as he was led around, in order to discourage his temperamental tendencies. Aureole, too, was susceptible to mental problems and he became overwrought by the occasion, breaking out in a nervous sweat before the parade began.

The race itself proved remarkably uneventful, considering the fact that there were 27 starters. The hopeless outsider City

Scandal showed the way for the first furlong and a half, but gave way there to Shikampur, the mount of one of fortune's Derby favourites, Charlie Smirke (he had already won three times and would add a fourth in 1958). This, though, was not to be Smirke's day, despite the strong gallop he set on the Aga Khan's colt.

Richards, who had been drawn close to the inside, met no problems on Pinza. The colt found a position on the rails, maybe no nearer than twelfth after three furlongs, but going easily and keeping out of trouble. By the top of the hill, half-distance, he was up to fifth or sixth, and when the descent to Tattenham Corner came, he was clearly in the ideal position from which to launch his bid.

Of course, it was at this point that many expected Pinza to falter. His vast, cumbersome frame was never built for the twists and climbs and drops of Epsom's switchback circuit. But the critics were confounded as the great, long-striding colt continued to move as sweetly as ever – even gaining ground and places as he negotiated the contours as handily as a polo pony.

When they came into the straight, only Shikampur lay between Pinza and victory. There were still three or four lengths to retrieve in those last three and half furlongs, but there was already no threat from the rear. Pinza's acceleration downhill had effectively outclassed all his pursuers; his stamina could be taken on trust.

Shikampur battled on well, but he was at the end of his tether with more than two furlongs to run. Gordon – *Sir* Gordon, as all the world now knew – was going to win the Derby! Pinza flashed by Shikampur with scarcely a movement from his jockey. Then, with every succeeding bound, he underlined his superiority. There were four lengths to spare at the finish, by which time Aureole had burst through to snatch a meritorious second place.

The reception for the winner was rapturous – partly, no doubt, for a very high-class horse, but principally for the great little man who had thrilled two generations by his uncanny talents and captured their hearts by his marvellous sportsmanship. Only now was he sampling that supreme moment in a jockey's career; the knighthood would not have to be regarded as consolation for 28 failures!

Richards himself seemed uncommonly subdued, as though a Derby victory was so strange to him that he did not know how he was supposed to react. Several minutes elapsed before he could express his emotions, for the affection shown him by the spectators overwhelmed him and left his brain numbed. Modest as ever, he was simply embarrassed to witness his own popularity and the sanctuary of the weighing room was a blessed relief.

Horse racing has a habit of bringing people rapidly back to earth and Gordon came down from the clouds by getting beaten on hot favourites in the next two races. But the victory on Pinza, and the subsequent interview with the Queen (who seemed as delighted with the result as if her own colt had won) made June 6 1953 the happiest day for a much-loved knight.

Pinza raced only once more (beating Aureole again in the King George VI and Queen Elizabeth Stakes at Ascot) before his malformed forelegs gave up the unequal struggle of trying to support his massive weight at racing pace.

Nobody knew it at the time, but Pinza had been Sir Gordon's last Derby chance. After being champion jockey for the 26th time in 1953, the youthful 50-year-old suffered two injuries in 1954. The first kept him out of the Derby, and the second caused the announcement of his retirement on August 10. That old cliché 'end of an era' really applied.

DERBY STAKES. At Epsom, Saturday, 6 June 1953. $1\frac{1}{2}$ miles. £19,118 to the winner. For 3-year-olds only.

Sir V. Sassoon's b.c. Pinza. 9st 0lb   Sir G. Richards   1
H.M. Queen Elizabeth II's ch.c. Aureole. 9st 0lb
                                              W. H. Carr   2
Prince Said Toussoun's b.c. Pink Horse. 9st 0lb
                                              W. R. Johnstone   3
H. H. Aga Khan's ch.c. Shikampur. 9st 0lb   C. Smirke   4
L. B. Holliday's b.c. Chatsworth. 9st 0lb   S. Clayton   5
M. Boussac's b.c. Pharel. 9st 0lb   J. Doyasbère   6
F. W. Dennis's b.c. Timberland. 9st 0lb   G. Littlewood   7
Lady Bullough's ch.c. Prince Canarina. 9st 0lb E. C. Elliott   8
W. Humble's b.c. Nearula. 9st 0lb   E. Britt   9
R. S. Clark's ch.c. Good Brandy. 9st 0lb   D. Smith   10
J. E. Ferguson's b.c. Mountain King. 9st 0lb   T. Gosling   11
Mrs G. Alderman's ch.c. Windy. 9st 0lb   F. Barlow   12
J. G. Morrison's br.c. Fellermelad. 9st 0lb   A. Breasley   13

Lord Milford's br.c. Empire Honey. 9st o1b   W. Rickaby 14
L. Lipton's ch.c. Prince Charlemagne. 9st o1b   L. Piggott 15
J. McGrath's b.c. Novarullah. 9st o1b   C. Spares 16
F. W. Dennis's br.c. Durham Castle. 9st o1b   A. Roberts
C. Wijesinghe's b.c. Jaffa. 9st o1b   J. Egan
H. S. Lester's ch.c. Gala Performance. 9st o1b   E. Mercer
Ley On's b.c. Fe Shaing. 9st o1b   S. Wragg
Lord Londonderry's b.c. Scipio. 9st o1b   J. Lindley
J. Olding's br.c. Victory Roll. 9st o1b   M. Beary
C. H. Rodwell's b. or br.c. Peter-so-Gay. 9st o1b P. Evans
W. Preston's b.c. Star of the Forest. 9st o1b   K. Gethin
W. P. Wyatt's b.c. Premonition. 9st o1b   E. Smith
Lord Antrim's b.c. City Scandal. 9st o1b   A. P. Taylor
N. W. Purvis's b.c. Barrowby Court. 9st o1b   T. Carter 27

Winner bred by F. Darling. Trained by N. Bertie.

Betting: 5–1 Pinza, Premonition, 9–1 Aureole, 10–1 Nearula, 100–8 Good Brandy, Novarullah, 100–6 Chatsworth, Shikampur, 22–1 Pharel, Fellermelad, Star of the Forest, 33–1 Pink Horse, Mountain King, 40–1 Empire Honey, 50–1 Prince Canarina, Victory Roll, 66–1 Prince Charlemagne, 100–1 others.

Won by 4 lengths, 1½ lengths. Time: 2min 35.6sec.

PRIX DE L'ARC DE TRIOMPHE, LONGCHAMP, FRANCE, OCTOBER 7 1956

RIBOT

*when an unbeaten international champion bade a glorious
farewell to the racecourse*

Racing and breeding in Italy, the youngest of the big thoroughbred powers, have flourished during the last 50 years in
remarkable circumstances. Her breeding industry has never
been developed on a scale similar to that in England, France,
or Ireland, and even now the number of mares at stud in Italy
represents no more than a tiny fraction of the total in any one
of the other three countries.

Defying the widely held belief that there can be no quality
without quantity, Italy manages to produce from its limited
resources a steady flow of horses capable of running with
distinction in international competition. More remarkably,
just occasionally she is able to raise horses of the very highest
calibre – animals capable not only of matching the best from
abroad, but also of setting new standards of performance
while beating them.

Apelle (Coronation Cup), Ortello (Prix de l'Arc de Triomphe), Crapom (Prix de l'Arc de Triomphe), and Tofanella
(Braunes Band von Deutschland) in the late 1920s and early
1930s were among the first representatives of Italian stables
to achieve international recognition. They were followed by
two products of the Razza Dormello-Olgiata who were to
wield enormous influence as stallions after magnificent racing
careers. Donatello was unluckily beaten in the 1937 Grand
Prix de Paris (his only defeat), but his stable companion
Nearco more than made up for that disappointment by landing
the same prize in 1938, with the English and French Derby
winners among his victims.

Nearco was bought for £60,000 to take up stud duties in
England, where he became leading sire on two occasions and
founded the male line which was to dominate classic pedigrees
world-wide until the present day. Winner of all his 14 starts

(the first 13 at home), Nearco represented the supreme achievement of Italian breeding until, on February 27 1952, there arrived a foal who was destined to eclipse him as a racehorse and rival him as a stallion.

The new champion was Ribot, an Italian folk hero for whom Fate decreed a most unlikely birthplace – West Grinstead, Sussex. It was here that the old English National Stud was located and here that Tenerani, the sire of Ribot, was stationed in 1952, when Romanella came to join his harem. The pair had been mated in Italy the previous year and her owner-breeder was confident enough about the as yet unborn offspring to want to repeat the union, even though it meant a long journey for the pregnant mother.

But Federico Tesio was more than Romanella's owner-breeder. He was also the owner-breeder of Tenerani, whom he had trained to a host of victories, including the 1948 Goodwood Cup. Moreover, Tesio was a genius – perhaps the only thoroughbred breeder who ever merited the epithet.

In 1951, when Ribot was conceived, a colt called Daumier became the twentieth Tesio-bred winner of the Derby Italiano. The list includes the aforementioned Apelle, Donatello, Nearco, and Tenerani. For long periods, Tesio *was* Italian racing and breeding; he established and maintained his reputation with a series of judicious purchases and shrewd matings. The success of his policy was uncanny – no wonder that he acquired the nickname 'Wizard of Dormello'.

The production of Ribot affords a typical astonishing example. Tenerani's dam Tofanella was bought as a yearling at Doncaster for 140 guineas; Romanella's dam Barbara Burrini was acquired as a foal at Newmarket for 350 guineas. Nobody in the history of the thoroughbred ever converted cheap stock into champions as consistently as Federico Tesio.

When Ribot was foaled, and for many months thereafter, there was nothing to suggest that one of the wonders of the equine world had been created. He was returned to Italy with his dam (again pregnant, but this time with a filly destined never to race) and even Tesio was not very impressed with him. As a foal and as a yearling the colt seemed as insignificant as he was small. Because of his tardy growth, Ribot was not entered in the Italian classic races for three-year-olds – a catastrophic blunder which showed that even the 'wizard' was human.

Because of his lack of size, Ribot acquired the nickname *il piccolo* (the little one), but his intelligence and activity convinced at least one person – stable-lad Mario Marchesi – that he would make a name for himself. Marchesi, a middle-aged man who had been with Tesio for many years, did not care if his superiors preferred the well-grown types like Derain and Audran. The spirit and character of *il piccolo* would assert themselves in time and when they did, all the physical attributes of Derain, Audran, and the like would be worthless by comparison. Of course, all stable lads talk like that when the new intake of yearlings arrives – the sense of optimism and spirit of rivalry *must* be there or the horse will never stand a chance – but on this occasion Marchesi had the tackle to make good his boast.

After having been so much more backward than his contemporaries, Ribot made swift progress when put into serious training. By April 1954, Tesio was convinced that this colt's style of galloping made him the pick of the crop, a potential champion in the Nearco class. But the old man did not live to see his prediction fulfilled; he died on May 1, a little over two months before Ribot made his first appearance on the racecourse.

Although the presiding genius had departed, the Razza Dormello-Olgiata operation continued on the same lines, with the widow, Donna Lydia Tesio, in half-shares with the Marchese Mario Incisa della Rocchetta. The latter was officially the trainer, though head man Ugo Penco provided the real professional expertise in that department, and he it was who stripped Ribot for his first public outing in the Premio Tramuschio at San Siro, Milan. The colt won comfortably by a length from his stable companion Donata Veneziana, without revealing anything like his true merit.

That merit became rather more apparent in his other two races that season, when he beat Zenodoto by two lengths in the Criterium Nazionale and followed with a narrow victory over Gail in the Gran Criterium. If the last success, by only a head, did not seem very convincing at the time, it looked a lot better after Gail had beaten good older horses in the valuable Premio Chiusura three weeks later.

Having been champion at two, Ribot never looked like relinquishing his title in his second season, even though he held no classic engagements. He opened his campaign by beating Donata Veneziana six lengths in the Premio Pisa,

The 1913 Derby brought Emily Davison's last desperate act in the cause of women's suffrage. *Above*, she greets the King's colt Anmer with open arms, and *below*, the inevitable has occurred.

Epsom Downs were packed to capacity when Sir Gordon Richards finally won the Derby — at the 28th attempt. It was Coronation Year, 1953, and the horse was Pinza.

The last racing photograph of Ribot. Jockey Enrico Camici searches for the opposition at the finish of the 1956 Prix de l'Arc de Triomphe, climax of the Italian colt's unbeaten career.

Kelso stands garlanded in the winner's circle after the 1964 Washington D.C. International, in which he ran the fastest mile-and-a-half in history.

The 1965 Prix de l'Arc de Triomphe attracted the finest field ever assembled for an international weight-for-age classic. This is how Sea-Bird treated them.

5 Gombos

3 Pentland Firth 50-1

4 Our Mirage

1 Roberto 3-1 fav.

2 Rheingold 22-1

Lester Piggott's sixth Derby victory came with Roberto, whom he 'lifted' over the line to beat Rheingold by a short head in 1972.

Crisp (rails) led the field a merry dance almost throughout the 4¼ miles of the 1973 Grand National, but Red Rum collared him ten yards from the finish.

Secretariat's jockey, Ron Turcotte looks for his rivals in the 1973 Belmont Stakes, but they are way back down the track, and Ron can concentrate on beating the clock. 'Big Red' responds in magnificent style.

then thrashed Gail and Derain by ten lengths and five lengths in the semi-classic Premio Emanuele Filiberto.

Ribot came back lame after that race with a fetlock injury, then caught a cough and it was almost three months before he returned for a comfortable win over Derain in the Premio Brembo. Six weeks later he beat the same rival by ten lengths in another minor event. His form showed him to be far and away the best three-year-old in Italy (Derain was good enough to win the St Leger Italiano), so he had to be given the chance to prove his quality in top international company – the Prix de l'Arc de Triomphe.

Leaving nothing to chance, the Ribot camp decided to stage a full-scale trial over San Siro's 2400 metres (mile and a half) course. The three-year-old was galloped flat out with the four-year-old Botticelli, winner of the 1954 Derby Italiano and 1955 Ascot Gold Cup, and the young one came home the winner, hard held, by four lengths in fast time.

The French, while prepared to accept Ribot as a high-class horse in his own country, preferred to trust home form and the invader was allowed to start at almost 9–1. There was never a doubt about the result, for Enrico Camici (Ribot's rider throughout his career) had Tenerani's son among the leaders all the way, sent him clear early in the straight, and brought him home with three easy lengths to spare over Beau Prince.

Ribot now returned home for Italy's own minor version of the 'Arc', the Gran Premio del Jockey Club, which provided France with a chance to gain her revenge. Surprisingly, in view of the way Ribot had treated the French horses on their own territory, there were four who were brave enough to take up the challenge. One of them was Norman, who had not run at Longchamp, but who had won the Milan event in each of the last two years. Norman got nearest, but Ribot dealt him a crushing defeat, pulling away over the last three furlongs to win by 15 lengths. Believe it or not, Ribot was still on the upgrade!

Ribot's first three outings in 1956 brought easy wins in modest events, whereupon it was announced that he would be aimed at Britain's principal weight-for-age contest, the mile and a half King George VI & Queen Elizabeth Stakes at Ascot. But in the meantime he was subjected to an unusual preliminary – taking on the best home runners in the Gran Premio di Milano over the metric equivalent of one mile, seven furlongs. The Gran Premio d'Italia winner Tissot and the first two from the recent Derby Italiano, Barba Toni and Vittor Pisani, were all in the field, but Ribot slaughtered them for speed and stamina to win by eight lengths.

Ribot thus came to Ascot with 13 consecutive victories to his credit and he extended his sequence to 14 with what has been described as the least impressive win of his career. Certainly the heavy ground unsettled him and Camici found himself forced to push the champion along almost from the start, but Ribot ran all his rivals into the ground well before the finish, drawing comfortably away without quickening appreciably to beat High Veldt by five lengths. That may have seemed unimpressive, but not until Mill Reef came home six lengths clear of Ortis in 1971 was Ribot's winning margin in Ascot's prestige prize eclipsed.

If he had appeared sluggish at Ascot, no such complaint could be made about his next performance. In the Premio del Piazzale he was confronted by Magabit, winner of the Italian counterpart to the 2000 Guineas, over a distance – 1800 metres – calculated to favour his rival. But Camici took Ribot straight to the front, maintained a lead of about two lengths until the final 200 metres, then asked his mount to quicken. The effect was electrifying, for though Magabit never slowed, Ribot passed the post eight lengths clear, then covered another 11-second furlong while Camici tried vainly to pull him up!

Only one objective remained to crown the perfect racecourse career – a second victory in the Prix de l'Arc de Triomphe. Four horses, Ksar (1921 and 1922), Motrico (1930 and 1932), Corrida (1936 and 1937) and Tantiéme (1950 and 1951) had accomplished the feat before, but none since the race acquired its reputation as the world's premier horse-race. In the last few years, the 'Arc' had become the most competitive event anywhere in the five continents and the prestige it carried was worth two or three Derbys.

In 1956, the 20 runners set a new standard for all-round ability. The horses who lined up to do battle with Ribot included winners of the Washington International (Fisherman), Irish Derby (Talgo and Zarathustra), Oaks (Sicarelle), French Oaks (Apollonia), Grand Prix de Paris (Vattel), French St Leger (Arabian), Prix Lupin (Tanerko) and Grand Prix de Saint-Cloud (Burgos and Oroso), plus a runner-up in the Belmont Stakes (Career Boy). Little over a month after the event, Master Boing would add another Washington International and in the course of the next two seasons Oroso would win a Prix de l'Arc de Triomphe, Tanerko two Grands Prix de Saint-Cloud, and Zarathustra an Ascot Gold Cup.

Even a horse as demonstrably brilliant as Ribot ought to have been fully tested by that array of talent. The fact that he was not represents an enormous tribute to a magnificent racehorse; it is inconceivable that all his rivals suffered an 'off' day.

Besides, it was not the bare fact that Ribot beat them that mattered; nor even was it that this was his sixteenth consecutive victory. What was significant was the way it was achieved – and that here, on the greatest racing occasion of the year, before the most cosmopolitan racing audience of the year, the greatest racehorse of his era was *seen* to join the immortals.

Camici knew his horse well, as he was entitled to, and he played this farewell performance to the gallery. So confident of success, the jockey treated the whole affair like an exhibition, and it was stage-managed to perfection. When the action was complete, everybody knew that they had seen star quality of a calibre unsurpassed in their lifetime.

After an excellent level start, the American five-year-old, Fisherman, was driven into a long lead, jockey Sam Boulmetis pumping vigorously in characteristic US all-action style. Camici sat still with Ribot, holding third place while only cantering.

By halfway Fisherman's lead had been reduced by the French four-year-old Norfolk, but he had to be scrubbed along by Freddie Palmer to make up the leeway. Ribot remained third, still cantering, and Camici viewed the proceedings in front of him with some amusement.

There was Norfolk, no better than a good-class handicapper himself, flat out in an effort to make the pace for his stable companion Tenarèze – and he could not even get into the lead! And up front was Fisherman, a winner of the Washington International sacrificed to make the running for the other Whitney colour-bearer, Career Boy. Did they seriously believe that a strong gallop would upset the mighty Ribot? He was better equipped to cope with those tactics than any horse in history. But Camici would let them preserve their illusions a while longer.

Coming down the hill towards the home turn, Norfolk gave up the vain chase and Ribot cruised past him, though his rider remained blissfully unconcerned about Fisherman's long lead. He was certain that exhaustion would soon bring Fisherman back to Ribot; there was no need for the champion to exert himself.

Sure enough, as they swung right-handed up the final stretch Fisherman weakened visibly and Ribot came almost alongside. Camici had given him an inch more rein now and he was so obviously the winner at that stage, with about two and a half furlongs still to run, that a referee would have declared 'no contest'. Tanerko, Apollonia, and Talgo pursued the leading pair and in the following group came Career Boy, whose jockey did not have the best of views of Ribot and who still clung to thoughts of victory. But not for long.

Career Boy's pilot was Eddie Arcaro, greatest of all American jockeys, and he described the ensuing moments graphically: 'I was going along there pretty good, fast enough to win it, I thought, when all of a sudden – whoosh! A horse took off from me so fast I couldn't recognize him. That was Ribot.'

What Arcaro saw only as a blur shone like a beacon to the onlookers in the stands. Only a racehorse of the highest class could lie up with a strong pace in that company and then leave them like a bullet from a rifle. The speed he generated, with no visible encouragement from the saddle, had to be seen to be believed. There were top-class racehorses behind him, running on and giving of their best. But the acceleration Ribot produced would have made even Signor Ferrari proud – and the gear change was automatic!

Still on the bit, Ribot streaked effortlessly clear, but Camici elected not to check the wonder horse's glorious stride when the race was clearly won. This was his last race, and all the world had to know beyond doubt what manner of horse Italy, more particularly Tesio, had fashioned. They knew well enough by the time Ribot reached the post six lengths in front of Talgo, who in turn led Tanerko by two lengths.

The Longchamp crowd, often one of the world's most vitriolic, forgot that its own champion Apollonia had finished last. For even the most cynical, narrow-minded spectator could not remain unmoved when privileged to witness a super-horse in an epoch-making performance. 'We needs must love the highest when we see it.'

Now all the world recognized what little Mario Marchesi had known for three years – *il piccolo* was a star.

There was nothing left for Ribot to accomplish on the racecourse, but in deference to his legions of Italian fans, the four-year-old was given two exhibition gallops in his home country. The first was at San Siro, Milan, where he had run and won 12 times; the second took place at the Cappanelle, Rome's own racecourse, where, believe it or not, Italy's greatest champion never raced.

Displaying a keen sense of the theatrical, Ribot reserved for the Romans a treat no other racecourse crowd ever saw. He had finished his exhibition in splendid style, galloping well clear of stable companion Magistris; then, by way of accepting the cheers of the populace and expressing his vitality, he threw Camici. The jockey was uninjured, but if he had been hurt, I feel sure that the crowd's amusement would hardly have been diminished.

Spirit and character. Yes, Ribot had those qualities in abundance.

PRIX DE L ARC DE TRIOMPHE. At Longchamp, Sunday, 7 October 1956. 2400 metres. 29,515,000 francs to the winner. For 3-year-olds and up.

Marchese Incisa della Rocchetta's b.c. Ribot. 4yrs, 60kg
E. Camici   1
G. A. Oldham's b.c. Talgo. 3yrs, 55½kg   E. Mercer   2
F. Dupré's br.c. Tanerko. 3yrs, 55½kg   J. Doyasbére   3
C. V. Whitney's br.c. Career Boy. 3yrs, 55½kg   E. Arcaro   4
Mme A. E. Lombard's br.c. Master Boing. 3yrs, 55½kg
G. Chancelier   5
R. Meyer's br.c. Oroso. 3yrs, 55½kg   H. Signoret   6
M. Calmann's br.c. Fric. 4yrs, 60kg   B. Margueritte   7
R. Bedel's ch.c. Burgos. 4yrs, 60kg   Y. Parenti   8
C. V. Whitney's br.h. Fisherman. 5yrs, 60kg   S. Boulmetis   9
R. Beamonte's b.c. Arabian. 3yrs, 55½kg   J. Deforge   10
Prince Aly Khan's gr.c. Cobetto. 4yrs, 60kg   J. Massard
T. J. S. Gray's bl.h. Zarathustra. 5yrs, 60kg   W. H. Carr
J. Lignel's b.c. Norfolk. 4yrs, 60kg   F. Palmer
H. Baranez's b.c. Flying Flag. 3yrs, 55½kg   L. Heurteur
R. Boncour's ch.c. Saint Raphael. 3yrs, 55½kg   M. Larraun
Mme C. Del Duca's b.c. Ambiax. 3yrs, 55½kg
W. R. Johnstone
P. Duboscq's ch.c. Tenarèze. 3yrs, 55½kg   R. Poincelet
Mme L. Volterra's br.c. Vattel. 3yrs, 55½kg   M. Garcia
Mme L. Volterra's b.f. Sicarelle. 3yrs, 54kg   G. Lequeux
M. Boussac's br.f. Apollonia. 3yrs, 54kg   S. Boullenger 20

Winner bred by Razza Dormello-Olgiata. Trained by V. U. Penco.

Betting: 6–10 Ribot, 27–4 Apollonia, 8–1 Tanerko, 11–1 Vattel and Sicarelle (coupled), 19–1 Arabian, 21–1 Career Boy and Fisherman (coupled), 32–1 Fric, 33–1 Tenarèze, 37–1 Saint Raphael, 40–1 Burgos, 50–1 Zarathustra, 60–1 Norfolk, 75–1 Ambiax, 80–1 Cobetto, 100–1 Talgo, Master Boing, 120–1 Oroso, Flying Flag.

Won by 6 lengths, 2 lengths. Time: 2min 34.76sec.

KELSO

*when the world's most prolific earner set the seal on his
greatness*

Have you ever considered what is the most fiercely contested
prize in sport? The vision which soon springs to mind is that
of a cross-country race, many of which attract athletes in their
hundreds. The *Guinness Book of Records* suggests that the 1968
Nijmegen Vierdaagse march, in which 16,667 walkers took
part, established the all-time peak.

But America has provided an award for many years in which
there are, theoretically at least, many more competitors.
Racing there makes no concessions to the seasons and is held
somewhere on every one of the 365 days. The number of
horses who run during that period has exceeded 16,667 in
every year since 1946 and from that vast 'field' one, and one
only, is elected 'Horse of the Year'. On January 1 they are all in
with a chance; the winner does not have to defeat all the others
physically, but a grading system sorts out the talented from the
indifferent, and it is sheer merit which establishes the ultimate
hero in the highest class.

A Kentucky Derby, a Preakness Stakes, a Belmont Stakes,
or, for a filly, a Coaching Club of America Oaks, represent the
individual prizes most coveted by breeders, owners, trainers,
and jockeys in the USA. But consistency is the hallmark of
class, and championships, decided over a series of races, mean
far more than any 'one off' triumphs. A champion of champions – 'Horse of the Year' – is something really special, a pearl
beyond price.

Kelso was more than that. He was 'Horse of the Year'
for five consecutive seasons, dominating the American racing
scene more completely and for longer than any other runner
before or since. There were 29,773 in contention when Kelso
took his first crown in 1960. The numbers rose by stages to
30,381 in 1961, 33,579 in 1962, 35,828 in 1963, and 37,812

71

in 1964, but all these reinforcements were powerless to budge Kelso from his throne. He was undisputed king – and not until he had reached the venerable age of eight, when he raced an abbreviated three-month season and suffered an eye injury in his last start, was he prepared to abdicate.

Kelso won more money – $1,977,896 – than any other thoroughbred in history. He won at all distances from six furlongs to two miles. He won on dirt and grass, setting records on both surfaces, and it did not concern him whether the track was firm or heavy. He won on 12 different courses, with six different jockeys. He won in every calendar month apart from January, in which he raced only once, and April, when he did not run at all. Truly he was a horse for all courses and for all seasons. More than a 'Horse of the Year', he was surely the 'Horse of the Era'.

The story of Kelso really begins with his sire, Your Host, a grandson of the game and classy Hyperion, victor of the 1933 Epsom Derby and Doncaster St Leger. Your Host, or 'Old Sidewinder' as he was affectionately known, had won 13 races and accumulated $384,795 when he was brought down during the San Pasqual Handicap in January 1951. His off fore-leg was shattered in four places at the ulna (forearm), and, as there was the little matter of an insurance policy for $250,000 to be considered, a panel of veterinary surgeons was convened to determine whether he could be saved. In common with many other learned bodies before and since, they argued long and hard, but came to no conclusions. The unprecedented result of their dithering was that after two months the insurers, Lloyds of London, paid off the full amount of the policy to owner William Goetz, but did not destroy the horse. Instead, they put him to stud themselves in California for a season, then sold him for $150,000 to a group of New Jersey breeders whose members included Mrs Richard C. duPont, owner of Woodstock Farm in Maryland.

Mrs duPont joined the syndicate because she was immensely impressed not only by Your Host's racetrack prowess, but also by the fortitude he displayed in his long and painful ordeal. Courage, a quality she valued highly in a horse, was something apparently missing from Mrs duPont's mare Maid of Flight, who won three minor races but never seemed to get over a minor accident as a three-year-old. Your Host seemed the ideal mate, and Kelso was the result of their first union.

During his first season in training, when he was backward

in condition and most unimpressive to behold, Kelso was handled by a veterinary surgeon, Dr John M. Lee. He it was who advised Mrs duPont that the colt should be gelded, and he it was who performed the operation. In after years, when Kelso was carrying all before him at the races, an ill-informed cross-section of the public regretted, criticized, and condemned what the good doctor had done. 'The greatest racehorse America has produced, deprived of the power to pass on his gifts – it was tantamount to murder' was one typical remark.

The fans who wanted to bury Lee should have praised him, for Kelso would never have aspired to racing's 'Hall of Fame' as an entire horse. The way Lee saw it, as his vet and trainer, there was no alternative. 'Kelso's reproductive organs interfered with his action', he recalled. 'The only way he could make a racehorse was to be castrated, and the results speak for themselves.'

Under Lee's tutelage, Kelso raced only three times before a stifle injury intervened. All those starts were at the Atlantic City track in New Jersey and he won the first, a maiden event, at odds of 6–1. Never, in 62 more lifetime starts, was he to start at such remunerative odds again; in no fewer than 53 of those races he would be favourite.

He finished second in each of his other two races as a juvenile, then suffered the mishap which kept him out of the three-year-old classics. Yet those nine months away from the racecourse may have been a blessing in disguise, for Kelso was able to fill out and develop his strength naturally, without being subjected to the strict regimen of the training stable. He came back, now trained by old-time jockey, Carl Hanford, to win minor events at Monmouth Park and Aqueduct by ten lengths and 12 lengths respectively before being shipped out to Illinois for the Arlington Classic, in which he ran a dull eighth. It seemed he might be just one of those good horses who narrowly missed the top bracket.

'King Kelly', as he was to become, soon corrected that impression, putting together a skein of 11 victories to remain unbeaten for 13 months. Despite his late start to the campaign, he was elected 1960 'Horse of the Year' by a comfortable margin, clinching his title with a record-breaking effort in the two-mile Jockey Club Gold Cup at Aqueduct, a race he was to make his own for five seasons.

There was never much doubt that Kelso would retain his

title in 1961, for by the end of July he had annexed the so-called Handicap Triple Crown, a feat previously attained only by Whisk Broom in 1913 and Tom Fool in 1953. 'Handicapper' may be a somewhat derogatory term in the British Isles, but its connotation is flattering in the USA, for handicaps represent the logical progression after the completion of the classic series.

By his victories in the Triple Crown of Metropolitan, Suburban, and Brooklyn, all run at Aqueduct, just a dozen miles from mid-Manhattan, Kelso became established as the idol of every New Yorker. He was also 'adopted' by a vast following throughout the eastern seaboard states, where nearly all his races took place. An organized fan club rapidly acquired a flourishing membership, the news media featured him copiously and, of course, his name was exploited *ad nauseam*. Finally the commercialism reached the stage where you could buy sugar lumps in wrappings of yellow and grey (the racing colours of Mrs duPont's Bohemia Stable), with miniature portraits of Kelso in the middle.

But all this commercialism was justifiable, for it reflected genuine interest in, and affection for, a magnificent horse, even though some old-timers were far from convinced of his pre-eminence. Kelso's deeds, they reckoned, still did not match those recorded by brilliant geldings of former days, like Exterminator, Old Rosebud, Roamer, and Armed. Maybe they were right; but time was on Kelso's side.

It was at the end of 1961 when Kelso first tried a grass surface. His first 20 races had all been on dirt, but an invitation to the Washington International, with the allure of its $70,000 first prize, was an almost literal back-handed compliment it was hard to refuse. The International, brainchild of John Schapiro, was devised in 1952 with the declared object of bringing together the world's greatest horses over the classic distance of a mile and a half at the end of the year, when most would have completed their parochial campaigns. In deference to the 'backward' Europeans, grass was the chosen surface and for the first 13 runnings the start was effected from the old-fashioned tape. It was hard luck on the American dirt runners who had never started from anything but stalls, but Schapiro knew that he would never attract a top European horse without making those concessions.

Top European horses did come, but in 1961 only the French colt Misti appeared to have any chance against the American

74

pair, Kelso and TV Lark, who dominated the betting and the race. This was the tenth International and only one favourite, Bald Eagle in 1960, had so far won. Kelso started at 2–5, but he could not improve that ratio, going under by three-quarters of a length to his compatriot, who had previous experience of racing on turf. Poor Kelso set a brisk pace until losing his advantage at the furlong pole, rallied to force TV Lark to a race-record time, then pulled up with sprains in fore- and hind-legs which kept him out of racing for well over six months.

There were six victories from 12 starts in Kelso's 1962 campaign, including the Woodward Stakes, the Jockey Club Gold Cup (inevitably), and a very minor event on grass at Saratoga. However, Beau Purple beat him over turf in the Man o' War Stakes and when the International came around again, the betting foreshadowed a repeat of that result. It did not turn out that way, for after the two had rocketed away from the tapes like bats out of hell, Kelso beat Beau Purple into submission in seven furlongs. The gelding next repulsed a powerful challenge from the 1961 Kentucky Derby winner Carry Back, establishing his mastery over that rival before the entrance to the straight. But then along came Match, winner of the Grand Prix de Saint-Cloud and the King George VI & Queen Elizabeth Stakes earlier that season, to pounce on the exhausted Kelso in the dying strides.

Kelso took his earnings past the $1,000,000 mark when he won his only subsequent 1962 start, and in 1963 he proved better than ever. Nine victories and two second places from 12 outings brought his biggest seasonal haul of $569,762, including eight consecutive wins between March and October. Then came his third attempt at Laurel and his first effort on grass since his previous year's failure. Again he found one too good, chasing his countryman Mongo throughout the last mile but never quite getting to him.

As a 'grand old man' of seven, Kelso ought to have been deteriorating by 1964. It seemed that this might indeed be the case when he flopped into eighth and sixth places in his first two starts, both at Hollywood Park – the only venture of his life to the west coast. Carl Hanford swiftly decided that California did not agree with the gelding and he shipped Kelso back to New York, where he promptly won a handicap under 9st 10lb in impressive style. He was clearly as good as ever in his own neck of the woods.

However, three defeats followed, behind Iron Peg, Mongo, and Gun Bow. All three received allowances of weight and the first two beat him only in photo-finishes, but Gun Bow had a wide margin to spare after Kelso hit his head on the starting stall and raced in a dazed condition throughout.

Kelso now equalled the American record for nine furlongs on grass in a minor event before crossing swords again with Gun Bow in the Aqueduct Stakes. Kelso gained his revenge here at level weights, but a month later the decision was reversed once more on the same terms in the Woodward Stakes, which Kelso was trying to win for the fourth year running. Gun Bow gained a nose verdict after one of the most thrilling duels ever witnessed up the straight at 'Big A', the judges taking more than five minutes to decipher an enlargement of the photo-finish print.

Four weeks later Kelso came out none the worse to score his fifth consecutive triumph in the Jockey Club Gold Cup. As he stormed home by $5\frac{1}{2}$ lengths and more from that season's American Derby winner Roman Brother and Belmont Stakes winner Quadrangle, Kelso surpassed the earnings of Round Table to become, in the American's curious approximation of the English language, the world's 'winningest' horse. He also broke the US two-mile record he himself had set in this same race four years previously.

And so to Maryland. As he had failed in three Internationals already, it was surely expecting too much of the old fellow to carry off the laurels at the age of seven. Yet he had just indicated his well-being by scoring one of the very best victories of his life. Everyone willed him to win, and sentiment made him the favourite at 6–5.

The annual game of 'Which one will beat Kelso at Laurel?' produced a natural choice in Gun Bow. He had won the Charles H. Strub, Whitney and Woodward Stakes, the San Antonio, Gulfstream Park, Brooklyn and Washington Handicaps. What is more, two of those successes were gained at the expense of the old warrior himself, and victory here would guarantee the 'Horse of the Year' title for Gun Bow. He was backed at 6–4.

Give John Schapiro credit. He had also induced classic horses from Russia, Ireland, France, Argentina, Italy, and Japan. But everybody seemed to know that this International concerned only the home team; the needle match with the championship at stake cornered all the attention.

For once, the pundits and the public were right. The six foreigners might as well have stayed at home for all the involvement that they had in this stupendous trial of strength. The blinkered, tearaway front-runner Gun Bow, with dual champion jockey Walter Blum in the saddle, burst away from the tapes with Kelso in hot pursuit, though settling well for his pilot, Ismael ('Milo') Valenzuela. The others could lurk at the back and settle their own trivial contest; for the entire mile and a half, there were two distinct races in progress, with never a prospect of a merger.

As they passed the stands for the first time, Gun Bow stretched out impressively in front, four lengths clear of Kelso. Belle Sicambre led the second division from Biscayne and Anilin, although that fact was already irrelevant. The track was hard and fast, ideally suited to a speed-merchant of Gun Bow's stamp, and when the first half-mile was completed in under 47 seconds it was clear that a record time was on the cards.

In the back straight the first pair maintained their blistering gallop, apparently intent on running each other to a standstill. Both were reputed to suffer from delicate feet, but nobody would have guessed it as their hooves pounded turf as firm as the runway at Idlewild. Legs of steel were required to withstand the jarring caused by shifting half a ton of body weight at racing pace on that surface. Neither hero flinched from his task.

Having ridden seven of the fastest furlongs of his life, Walter Blum must have been staggered to watch Milo Valenzuela bring Kelso smoothly alongside, then further demoralized to see the old champion edge ahead. When the mile mark was reached Kelso had a narrow advantage, and the time was little more than a second outside the world record. And there was half a mile still to run!

As they approached the home turn, a mile and a quarter accomplished in two minutes flat, the duet became a solo. Gun Bow had given his all, but it was not enough. He tired visibly, brushed Kelso slightly, then may have been inconvenienced momentarily as his rival moved across. Blum continued to egg him on with hands and heels, but Kelso was soon gone beyond recall, reaping the reward his consistency had earned him.

More important, he established his authority not simply by staying on more strongly than an exhausted opponent. Kelso was not slowing down by any means and though

Valenzuela applied nothing more vigorous than mild hand urgings, the gelding stopped the clock at 2 minutes 23.8 seconds, fracturing all manner of records, most notably the world's best at the distance.

Gun Bow plugged on gamely to finish four and a half lengths behind the champion, while the stragglers' contest, conducted nine and more lengths adrift of the principals, was won by the Russian colt Anilin, who produced a notable late surge to give notice that racing behind the Iron Curtain would soon have to be taken seriously.

Kelso was acclaimed rapturously by the crowd of nearly 38,000, who felt with good reason that the thirteenth running of the International had outshone all its predecessors. It may not have lived up to its name, but what a horse race!

The 1964 Washington International would have provided a fitting finale to Kelso's career. He had done it all now and nothing could dim the memory of his wonderful achievements. However, the gelding stood within striking distance of becoming the world's first $2,000,000 earner, so he was kept in training to pursue that target.

Mrs duPont neither wanted nor needed the cash. But she wanted the record for her beloved 'Kelly' and that seemed ample justification. As it happened, the old stager could not quite make it, though he kept his form amazingly well. An eye injury curtailed his activities in 1965 and in the following spring a hairline fracture of an off-fore sesamoid caused his final withdrawal from racing.

His owner retired him to her farm near Chesapeake City, where she hacked and hunted him after he had regained his soundness. I caught up with him there in 1970, almost six years to the day after his Laurel triumph. Elegant and intelligent, though necessarily a good deal tubbier than in his racing days, he evidently thrived on his new way of life and had proved a fluent and enthusiastic jumper.

A plaque set in the outer wall of his box proclaimed his achievements and called him 'The most durable horse in racing history'. Nobody would care to dispute that. But even more noticeable than the plaque was the condition of the lower door, marked, dented, obviously eaten away in places. Surely the great Kelso could not be a crib-biter? British trainers and breeders throw up their hands in horror at horses who display that vice, declare that all who do it are worthless and would not have one in their stables at any price.

Yes, I was told, Kelso was a crib-biter, and had been all his racing life. No doubt he was just another of those exceptions who prove a rule. But then Kelso was exceptional. Period,

---

WASHINGTON D.C. INTERNATIONAL. At Laurel, Maryland, USA, Wednesday, 11 November 1964. 1½ miles. $90,000 to the winner. For 3-year-olds and up.

Bohemia Stable's dk.b. or br.g. Kelso. 7yrs, 9st 0lb		
	I. Valenzuela	1
Gedney Farm's b.c. Gun Bow. 4yrs, 9st 0lb	W. Blum	2
Voskhod Stud's b.c. Anilin. 3yrs, 8st 10lb	N. Nasibov	3
Mrs J. Reid's b.c. Biscayne. 3yrs, 8st 10lb	W. Williamson	4
Mme L. Volterra's b.f. Belle Sicambre. 3yrs, 8st 7lb		
	L. Piggott	5
R. Fabris & S. Ledwith's ch.h. Primordial. 7yrs, 9st 0lb		
	L. Pincay, Jr	6
A. & M. Perego's ch.c. Veronese. 4yrs, 9st 0lb	F. Jovine	7
T. Miyoshi's b.h. Ryu Forel. 5yrs, 9st 0lb	I. Miyamoto	8

Winner bred by Mrs R. C. duPont. Trained by C. H. Hanford.

Betting: 6–5 Kelso, 6–4 Gun Bow, 52–10 Veronese, 172–10 Anilin, 262–10 Primordial, 295–10 Belle Sicambre, 354–10 Biscayne, 728–10 Ryu Forel.

Won by 4½ lengths, 9 lengths. Time: 2min 23.8sec.

PRIX DE L'ARC DE TRIOMPHE, LONGCHAMP, FRANCE, OCTOBER 3 1965

SEA-BIRD

when an Epsom Derby winner sprinted away from the Derby heroes of France, Ireland, America and Russia

Whenever the racing Press devotes space and attention to the question of the general merits of the present-day thoroughbred, there is always plenty of correspondence. The topic is raised only in a poor or mediocre year, so there is never an advocate for the modern horse. And, as everyone who has ever had so much as a 10p bet on a horse acknowledges himself as an expert on all matters equine (racing attracts the know-all rather more than any other sport), there is never a shortage of reasons why our stock has deteriorated.

One theory, though, predominates. It is churned out with the regularity of clockwork, but each new exponent delivers it with a resounding 'Eureka!' Reduced to its simplest terms, the message runs, 'We have been breeding from bad mares'. A number of exalted personalities have proposed some sort of test to determine whether a mare should or should not be used for breeding purposes – Lord Porchester suggested that only mares who were themselves winners should be employed.

The notion is nonsensical for more than theoretical reasons. It is not necessary to be a women's libber to see that the blame is wrongly attributed. While nature permits a mare to have only one foal (or make one mistake) a year, a stallion is allowed to beget forty or more offspring for several years running before it is realized that his influence is disastrous. In this instance, the female of the species is far less deadly than the male.

A shorter refutation of the anti-feminist propaganda comes in two syllables – Sea-Bird. In the opinion of many experienced observers, this French-bred colt was the 'Horse of the Century'; if any standards had been applied relating to his female ancestry, he would never have existed. His dam, Sicalade, could do no better than dead-heat once for second place; *her* dam, Marmelade, ran only once and was unplaced;

her dam, Couleur, was useless on the Flat, but won once over hurdles; *her* dam, Colour Bar, could manage no more than third in a selling race before winning under Pony Turf Club Rules; *her* dam, Lady Disdain, ran only twice and was unsuccessful. So for five generations the family proved all but worthless; the sixth generation produced what may have been the finest racehorse the world has ever seen.

Sea-Bird came into the world on March 8 1962, at the Haras de Victot, in the *département* of Calvados. His dam had been sent there to be covered by the resident stallion Beau Prince, but she had first to be delivered of the foal she carried by Dan Cupid, a horse who had finished a close second in the 1959 Prix du Jockey-Club (French Derby), only to disappoint on several other occasions.

It could hardly be said that the arrival of that foal was anticipated with baited breath, and afterwards the staff would recall the incident more for the fact that Sicalade was a very awkward mare than for any impression that they had assisted at the birth of a champion.

Sea-Bird was Sicalade's second foal, but the birth was no easier than her first a year before, when her colt Statu Quo arrived. The mare's problem was one of circulation, which caused her pain, risked infection, and cast doubts on her utility as a mother. She recovered well enough in 1962 and Sea-Bird did not seem to suffer unduly, but the trouble recurred in the following year when her Beau Prince colt Syncom was born, so that owner Jean Ternynck wondered whether she was really more bother than she was worth.

Ternynck, a wealthy industrialist from the wool centre of Roubaix, deferred a decision until November 1963, when he telephoned his trainer, Etienne Pollet, who was also a distant cousin. Together they reviewed the situation. The mare's first foal, Stato Quo, had not run and Pollet doubted whether he ever would; the second foal, Sea-Bird, seemed a nice sort of colt, but so do many at nineteen months of age, before they have been tested; the third foal, Syncom, was a far from impressive individual. Add to all that the fact that Sicalade was not pregnant, and the owner did not really need to ask the question. The only sensible course of action was to cut his losses.

Ternynck replaced the receiver, then contacted a butcher at Andelys, and Sicalade was promptly sold for the equivalent of £100. Two years later the mare would have been worth £100 for each pound of her body weight, but who could foresee what that leggy yearling in Pollet's Chantilly yard would become? And when that colt had outrun the world's next best thoroughbreds, who in Andelys would remember that they had eaten his dam? Pedigree does not count for much when served up on a plate.

Sea-Bird was not a quick developer, which was something of a disappointment to trainer Pollet. He had also handled the colt's sire, Dan Cupid, who was something of a flyer as a two-year-old, but the gangling chestnut son always indicated that he would require patience. Nevertheless, he was ready by September and he made a pleasing début when coming through late to win a modest event at Chantilly over 1400 metres by a short neck. A fortnight later he ran again over the same distance in the more important Criterium de Maisons-Laffitte and gave an almost identical performance. It did not seem a wonderful effort at the time; nobody had any idea that the runner-up, Blabla, would win the Prix de Diane (French Oaks) in the following year.

The first glimpse of the real Sea-Bird came in his third and last race as a two-year-old. Pollet's stable housed a far more precocious youngster called Grey Dawn that season, and his victories in the Prix Morny and Prix de la Salamandre indicated that he was probably the best of his generation. He was a natural favourite for the Grand Criterium, the 1600-metre Longchamp contest which annually decides the championship, but Pollet elected to run Sea-Bird as well, just to see how he shaped in top-class company.

Stable jockey Pat Glennon, a long-legged Australian who had ridden Sea-Bird to both his successes, understandably plumped for Grey Dawn this time, while the Dan Cupid colt was entrusted to Maurice Larraun, who was generally reliable if seldom inspired. Larraun rode Sea-Bird as though he knew Grey Dawn would win. He was right, for he let the favourite get so far ahead that success was always out of the question. Far from being able to swoop to victory with Sea-Bird, Larraun would have had trouble making up the leeway if he had been piloting Concorde. Grey Dawn beat him by two lengths, but many onlookers marked down the runner-up as the one to watch in 1965.

Sea-Bird was certainly the horse to watch throughout that year. There has never been another season in which the form of the top horses worked out so exactly, first locally, then throughout Europe, and finally in America. All the results pointed conclusively to the fact that Sea-Bird ruled the world.

Pollet gave the chesnut his first outing of 1965 in the Prix Greffulhe, a noted classic trial in which he was opposed by eight colts who had all been rated his inferiors as two-year-olds. Two of them, Corduroy and Pasquin, possibly held an advantage on the score of fitness, having run and won already that spring. They came home second and third, but could not cope with the explosive late surge of Sea-Bird, who drew right away in the last furlong and so impressed one London book-maker that his price for the Derby was reduced to 4-1. That was despite the fact that owner and trainer had not yet decided whether Sea-Bird would run at Epsom.

By the time of Sea-Bird's next race, the situation among the French three-year-olds was becoming interesting, to say the least. In the Prix Lupin, the most valuable and coveted of Derby trials, he had to contend with Diatome, who had just preserved his unbeaten record in the Prix Noailles, and Cambremont, who had won both his 1965 starts, including a shock victory over Sea-Bird's illustrious stable companion, Grey Dawn, in the Poule d'Essai des Poulains, France's equivalent of the 2000 Guineas.

These were surely formidable rivals, yet Sea-Bird brushed them nonchalantly aside with a furlong to run and cantered home with six lengths to spare over Diatome, who bested Cambremont by half a length after a struggle. Glennon re-ported that the winning margin would have been extended if he had not eased Sea-Bird in the last 100 yards. It was assuredly an awesome performance.

Within a few days Sea-Bird became a hot favourite for the Derby, his next objective. The Epsom classic has never been won more easily. Glennon had him lobbing along in a handy position throughout; brought him through, still cantering, to demolish the front-running I Say in a few loping strides; then pushed him out gently for a short distance to correct a tendency to idle. Sea-Bird was back 'on the bridle', cantering again, at the finish, where Meadow Court took second place, considerably flattered by a deficit of two lengths.

Sea-Bird's Derby win was clearly either a display of extra-ordinary merit, or his rivals were very moderate. That query was resolved in the next two months when Meadow Court beat 20 others comfortably in the Irish Sweeps Derby and followed with an equally convincing victory over the best older horses in the King George VI & Queen Elizabeth Stakes at Ascot. Meanwhile, Sea-Bird's runner-up in the Prix Lupin, Diatome, was earning excellent second places in France's top mid-season classics, the Prix du Jockey-Club and Grand Prix de Paris, beaten narrowly each time by a brilliant and unbeaten colt called Reliance.

Little over a fortnight after the Derby, a deal was concluded with the Kentucky breeder John W. Galbreath which was to take Sea-Bird to America for stud duty on a five-year lease and net Jean Ternynck about £500,000. The agreement stipulated that Sea-Bird could continue to race in Ternynck's bright green and black colours until the end of the season, so two more races were selected for him – the Grand Prix de Saint-Cloud and the Prix de l'Arc de Triomphe.

The Saint-Cloud race marked Sea-Bird's first excursion into open company. But the older horses ranged against him here could never get him to gallop, and he flashed past them in the straight without having to be asked. While they laboured, he was gliding, and Glennon kept the winning margin down to two and a half lengths, lest the others should die of shame!

Sea-Bird now withdrew from the public gaze for three months. He was perfectly sound, and capable of adding a lot more to his already healthy bank balance of something like £140,000. But the 'Arc' remained the only race which really mattered, and if Pollet, the supreme master of his craft in France, reckoned that the colt could be best prepared at home, that was good enough for Jean Ternynck. That is not to say, though, that those three months were not the longest of the owner's life.

Week after week came the nerve-racking knowledge that all the potential dangers to Sea-Bird in the 'Arc' were developing and ripening to fruition by the tried and trusted method of the racecourse test, while the champion stayed at home, thriving, it was true, but lacking that 'edge' which the spur of earnest competition confers.

When the great day arrived, Sea-Bird looked fit, eager, and overall a far more impressive specimen of the thoroughbred than he had been at any other time in his career. In the summer he had seemed a trifle spare; now he had gained weight and strength, his condition reflecting great credit on his trainer. But as the field cantered past the stands towards the start, the enormity of Sea-Bird's task seemed daunting. Was there ever such a collection of talent assembled for one race?

Preserving a precarious balance on a wall at the back of the old stand (the palatial facilities we know today were still to come), I ticked them off mentally as they passed me in racecard order. . . . Emerald, winner of the Prix Maurice de Nieuil last time out; Ardaban, third in the Prix Henri Foy; Anilin, the Soviet champion who had won the Russian Derby, 12 other races and had run third to Kelso at Laurel; Soderini, winner of the Hardwicke Stakes; Demi Deuil, recent victor of the Grosser Preis von Baden; Sigebert; winner of the Prix Henri Foy; Francilius, one contender who surely had no chance; Oncidium, England's chief hope and winner of the Coronation Cup; Timmy Lad, runner-up in the Grand Prix de Deauville; Free Ride, winner of the Prix Ganay, Greffulhe, and Hocquart; Diatome, hero of the Prix Noailles and du Prince d'Orange, runner-up in two classics; Meadow Court, victor of the Irish Sweeps Derby and King George VI & Queen Elizabeth Stakes; Khalife, his pacemaker; Carvin, winner of the Grand Prix de Vichy; Reliance, regarded as the principal threat to the favourite, unbeaten winner of five races including the Prix du Jockey-Club, Grand Prix de Paris and Prix Royal-Oak; Tom Rolfe, hero of the Preakness Stakes and American Derby, the outstanding three-year-old of the season in the USA; Ragazzo, second in the Prix Royal-Oak; Marco Visconti, second best of his age and sex in Italy; Sea-Bird himself; and the lone filly, Blabla, heroine of the Prix de Diane.

The day was sunny and warm, but there had been plenty of rain in the preceding week, so that the ground was decidedly soft. Sea-Bird, who had been sweating quite freely during the preliminaries, had never won on a similar surface, whereas Reliance had scored three of his successes on an easy terrain, something which must have been essential for probably the weirdest pair of forelegs owned by a top-class horse.

When the stalls opened, the slowest away was Khalife, which was something of an embarrassment to jockey Johnny Roe, whose orders were to set a strong pace for Meadow Court and Ragazzo. By dint of sheer hard labour, Roe forced Khalife into second place after a furlong, but he could never get his head in front, for Marco Visconti was working up a smooth rhythm in the lead and he had no intention of forfeiting his advantage just yet. Anilin surged forward to reach second place after two furlongs, displacing Khalife, who was pursued by Ardaban, Reliance, Tom Rolfe, and Sea-Bird.

The leading group remained much the same until they made the long descent towards the right-hand turn into the straight. Anilin now progressed to challenge Marco Visconti for the lead, with Ardaban third, ahead of Sea-Bird, who was clearly just marking time. The following group consisted of Emerald, Tom Rolfe, Khalife, Reliance, Sigebert, Meadow Court, and Carvin.

The effort of setting a strong pace in soft ground told on Marco Visconti at the entrance to the straight, where Anilin took over and behind him Sea-Bird and Reliance prepared to launch their bids. Now it was apparent that the showdown France had longed for all year was about to take place. Anilin, surely, would give way to let the Chantilly colts conduct their duel in private.

Obligingly, the Russian four-year-old did just that, retreating to the wings as the principals took centre stage. But even as it happened it was obvious that this duel would not last long, for one was simply playing with the other. Suddenly, with one rapier thrust, Reliance was left for dead.

Sea-Bird was granted an extra inch of rein and he took off as if jet-propelled. Pat Glennon, who had not even requested an effort, caught his breath at the most exhilarating moment of his life. Half the observers in the stands roared their enthusiasm. The other half were dumbfounded with incredulity.

This was Ribot all over again. Lying up with the pace, striking early in the straight – the formula was the same. But this time the quality of the beaten brigade was something special. It was no forlorn 100-1 shot like Talgo chasing Sea-Bird vainly up that straight. This was Reliance, himself a racehorse of the highest class, who had never been beaten before and who was here destroying eighteen of the world's top runners. Yet even as he established his massive superiority to them, he was himself being humiliated by a creature who, on that day, looked for all the world like the ultimate racehorse.

Throughout the last furlong Sea-Bird veered left, away from the rails, but so great was his advantage that Glennon did not even bother to correct him. He passed the post six lengths clear of the luckless Reliance, who himself had five lengths to spare over Diatome. Free Ride came late to deprive Anilin of fourth place, with Tom Rolfe – the best three-year-old in America – sixth, beaten over $16\frac{1}{2}$ lengths from the winner. It was six more lengths back to Demi Deuil in seventh place.

Sea-Bird had given, without doubt, the most devastating display of all time in an international weight-for-age classic. The comments of two of the participating riders are worth recording. From Willie Shoemaker, partner of Tom Rolfe: 'I kept looking over at that big dude (Sea-Bird) and the jock had a double nelson on him. He was going so nicely that I said to myself, I'd better get out of the way, because if that horse is ever turned loose he'll run over me.' From Pat Glennon, on being asked if he had ever ridden a better runner in his multi-national career, 'Sea-Bird is by far the best horse I have ever seen, let alone ridden.'

Thus closed the racing career of a phenomenon who set standards by which other horses will long be judged. In the six weeks after his retirement Anilin won Germany's top prize, the Preis von Europa, by four lengths, Diatome and Carvin finished first and second in the Washington International, and Demi Deuil ran away with the Premio Roma by seven lengths. The tributes to Sea-Bird from his fellow performers were as eloquent as those from horsemen and journalists.

Sea-Bird had fooled the 'experts' by becoming a superlative racehorse; he now proceeded to fool them all again by failing to become a superlative sire. By the time it was his turn to be dished up on a platter – all dead horses are converted into meat in France, regardless of their eminence – he had provided more than his share of ammunition for the argument that the principal reason for the existence of the horse is to teach man humility. Where racehorses are concerned, experts do not exist.

PRIX DE L'ARC DE TRIOMPHE. At Longchamp, Sunday, 3 October 1965. 2400 metres. 1,084,747 francs to the winner. For 3-year-olds and up.

J. Ternynck's ch.c. Sea-Bird. 3yrs, 55½kg   T. P. Glennon 1
F. Dupré's b.c. Reliance. 3yrs, 55½kg   Y. Saint-Martin 2
Baron G. de Rothschild's br.c. Diatome. 3yrs, 55½kg
J. Deforge 3
Baron G. de Rothschild's b.c. Free Ride. 4yrs, 60kg
L. Heurteur 4

Voskhod Stud's b.c. Anilin. 4yrs, 60kg   N. Nasibov 5
R. R. Guest's b.c. Tom Rolfe. 3yrs, 55½kg W. Shoemaker 6
A. Rueff's b.c. Demi Deuil. 4yrs, 60kg   H. Samani 7
J. Boutillier's b.c. Carvin. 3yrs, 55½kg   J. Massard 8
G. M. Bell's ch.c. Meadow Court. 3yrs, 55½kg L. Piggott 9
A. Palmieri's ch.c. Marco Visconti. 3yrs, 55½kg
                                                C. Marinelli 10
Mrs P. A. B. Widener's b.c. Timmy Lad. 4yrs, 60kg
                                                M. Larraun 11
M. Boussac's b.c. Emerald. 4yrs, 60kg   R. Poincelet 12
E. R. More O'Ferrall's b.c. Ragazzo. 3yrs, 55½kg J. Mercer 13
Mme L. Volterra's ch.c. Francilius, 4yrs, 60kg J. C. Desaint 14
Mme J. Stern's b.c. Sigebert. 4yrs, 60kg   F. Head 15
M. Boussac's b.c. Ardaban. 4yrs, 60kg   H. Mathelin 16
L. L. Lawrence's b.c. Soderini. 4yrs, 60kg   G. Lewis 17
Lord Howard de Walden's b.c. Oncidium. 4yrs, 60kg
                                                A. Breasley 18
G. M. Bell's ch.c. Khalife. 3yrs, 55½kg   J. Roe 19
G. Brun's ch.f. Blabla. 3yrs, 54kg   M. Depalmas 20

Winner bred by J. Ternynck. Trained by E. Pollet.

Betting: 6–5 Sea-Bird, 9–2 Reliance, 15–2 Diatome and
Free Ride (coupled), 31–4 Meadow Court and Khalife
(coupled), 8–1 Tom Rolfe, 22–1 Anilin, 23–1 Emerald and
Ardaban (coupled), 24–1 Blabla, 33–1 Ragazzo, 55–1 Marco
Visconti, 60–1 Demi Deuil, 70–1 Sigebert, 75–1 Oncidium,
Timmy Lad, 80–1 Carvin, 90–1 Soderini, 120–1 Francilius.

Won by 6 lengths, 5 lengths. Time: 2min 35.52sec.

ROBERTO

when the world's finest jockey produced his supreme effort
and equalled a 100-year-old record

Memories are notoriously short in racing. The horse popula-
tion is so vast and its turnover so fast that even the most
interested and involved find their recollections dimming,
distorting, and disappearing very quickly. It is a phenomenon
noticeable throughout the industry.

Breeders and trainers have great difficulty in recognizing
horses only a short time after they have left their care; jockeys
have to be interviewed immediately after a race, as half an
hour and one mount later they will remember little of what
happened and even less about any of the horse's characteristics.

Spend an hour or two in the company of old-time stable-lads
in Newmarket and you will feel tempted to make an exception
of this branch of the profession. They will regale you with
fascinating tales of personalities and performers so apparently
authentic that they seem to come virtually 'straight from the
horse's mouth'. But when you check the facts in the record
books, you will discover that your informant is invariably
wrong in almost every essential detail.

When you deal with hundreds or thousands of horses, it is
impossible to call up from memory all the salient facts about
one individual. If it is your unfortunate fate to handle only
run-of-the-mill performers all your life, your job may amount
to little more than a monotonous drudge on a slow-moving,
if animated, production line. Routine is simply not memorable.

Similarly with the punter. He will remember those horses
who have won any amount of money for him and those who
have cost him a large amount. He will also retain a vague
recollection of the really top-class performers he has seen,
plus those who have been involved in sensational events.

Greatness or notoriety – these are the only basic reasons why
individual horses are remembered at all by a wide public.
Yet there are those who fit into neither category and yet

deserve to be recalled – horses who, one way or another, influenced events which decidedly *were* memorable.

Take the case of The Broker. He was racing as recently as 1973, but how many people who were following the sport at that time have any recollection of him? There are bound to be a few punters who will remember the name, for he was a very disappointing horse who failed to live up to a high reputation – in fact he never won a race. One particular jockey could hardly forget him, but he will ring no bells for most people.

Nevertheless, this apparent nonentity earned a place in Turf history as surely as if he had won a classic. For he was the cause of, or the excuse for, the most bitter controversy on the domestic racing scene in 1972 and the most amazing finish to the Derby in generations. Thousands on the course and millions, via television, thrilled to those glorious moments. The Broker was responsible. And he did it all by falling over.

The vital incident occurred at Kempton Park on Saturday, May 27, when £807 was at stake for the Nassau Stakes, a minor event for three-year-olds. There were only five runners and the betting suggested that The Broker was only third best. As the field swung right-handed into the three-furlong straight, The Broker was last of the quintet, but moving sweetly, and his jockey, Bill Williamson, had not yet asked him for a serious effort.

The field closed up at the two-furlong marker, where all five contenders could be given a chance, then, with under 300 yards to go, it happened. Parthian Queen, who had led all the way, began to tire just as The Broker started a promising bid on her outside. The colt struck into the filly, came down and Williamson was catapulted from the saddle.

As the Australian jockey hit the turf, the first link was forged in a sensational chain of events which would stir the emotions of thousands in and out of racing. Anger, sorrow, bitterness, hate, compassion, admiration, and sheer wonder would all spring from this singular and apparently trivial incident.

Williamson was 49 years old, 35 years a jockey, a quiet man of enormous talent who inspired affection like few others in his profession. At home he had won almost every race worth winning, including the 1952 Melbourne Cup on Dalray. Since coming to Europe he had landed all the Irish classics at least twice (apart from the Sweeps Derby, which continued to elude him), the Newmarket 1000 Guineas twice, three French classics, plus two victories in the Prix de l'Arc de Triomphe. At this moment in time he stood on the threshold of an even greater triumph – the Epsom Derby – with the mount on Roberto, the favourite, eleven days hence. Enter The Broker. . . .

Williamson picked himself up from the Kempton turf, dusted himself off and started to check the damage. He had cuts about the face, but they were nothing to worry about; more significantly, he felt rather more than a little bit sore around the neck, shoulders and arms. While experience teaches you how to fall properly, age ensures that when those occasional tumbles occur they take more out of you. There was no question of his being able to ride again that day and he would have to place himself in the hands of the medical men.

There was alarmist talk about a possible broken collar-bone, an injury which does not mend easily when you are nearly fifty, but an x-ray over the weekend revealed no breakages. With the awesome responsibility of riding the Derby favourite obviously uttermost in his mind, Williamson decided to rest his aching body for a week, taking only a little light exercise before building up to peak fitness again with race-riding in Derby week itself.

When you reach Williamson's age without a Derby victory, you know your time is running out. He was already a few months older than Gordon Richards had been when Pinza won; he could hardly count on emulating his compatriot Scobie Breasley, who scored twice when in his fifties. What is more, Williamson knew full well that in Roberto he had a first-rate vehicle. The American-bred colt had won his first three races as a two-year-old in the style of a champion, had run below par in the Grand Criterium, but had returned at three to record two splendid efforts. In the Vauxhall Trial Stakes in Ireland he had notched a comfortable victory, then, ridden by Williamson for the first time, he had finished a meritorious second in the 2000 Guineas.

Roberto had been ridden by Johnny Roe, the stable jockey for trainer Vincent O'Brien, in his unbeaten career in Ireland. But Roe's sphere of activity did not stretch across the water and on their excursions to England and France, the representatives of the Ballydoyle stable were generally teamed with Lester Piggott. He it was who rode Roberto as a two-year-old

91

in France, where he finished fourth behind the aptly named Hard to Beat.

Piggott would certainly have been granted the option to ride Roberto in the 2000 Guineas but for a prior arrangement to partner the top 1971 two-year-old, Crowned Prince, for Bernard van Cutsem's stable. Crowned Prince, a most imposing individual who had always looked a champion, had been the favourite for the 2000 Guineas and the Derby all through the winter. Piggott made no secret of his belief that he was a racehorse of the highest class and the fact that he wanted to be associated with the colt in the 1972 classics.

Accordingly, Vincent O'Brien turned to Bill Williamson for the 2000 Guineas. The Australian's style could hardly have differed more from Piggott's, but 'Weary Willie', as everyone in racing knew him, was a big race specialist whose timing and artistry were faultless. His unhurried, unflurried manner was ideal for the great occasion and in previous battles with the Englishman they were about honours even. Piggott, with Ribero, had just pipped Williamson and Canterbury for the 1968 St Leger, and two years later he had driven Nijinsky past Gyr in the final furlong of the Derby. But the wily Aussie had proved one too good for Piggott in two Arcs de Triomphe, bringing Vaguely Noble home in front of Sir Ivor in 1968, then holding on with Levmoss against Park Top in 1969. There was even a school of thought in England which considered that Williamson was, taken all around, Piggott's superior; Piggott himself declared that the Australian was the hardest man in the world to beat.

Williamson, then, had Roberto for the Guineas, while Piggott was allied not to Crowned Prince, but to Grey Mirage, a winner of two classic trials yet considerably inferior to what most good judges regarded as true classic form. Crowned Prince, the supposed world-beater, had run ignominiously on his return to racing as a three-year-old and had been withdrawn from all engagements with a soft palate complaint.

High Top, the favourite, won the 2000 Guineas in splendid style, making all the running. He ran as straight as a gun barrel though a gale force wind and torrential rain oppressed him throughout. Grey Mirage wearied of the effort soon after halfway and dropped back to finish sixth, but Roberto made excellent late headway to claim second place, beaten only half a length. The third horse, Sun Prince, was six lengths away.

The bookmakers, who are rarely known for their generosity, suffered mental aberrations after the 2000 Guineas and offered odds of 8-1 against Roberto for the Derby. High Top was not entered at Epsom – he would not have stayed the distance in any case – while Roberto was expected to be more effective at a mile and a half. Most keen observers considered that 8-1 represented exceptional value, and none were more convinced than O'Brien and Williamson. They had, in a sense, plotted their own downfall at Newmarket, for the jockey had orders to restrain his mount's sometimes impetuous tendencies and he succeeded too well. Having idled for so long, Roberto took a while to rouse and got down to business too late.

After the Newmarket classic it crossed a few minds that Roberto would normally have been Piggott's mount, but for the infamous Crowned Prince, and that the English champion would now be available for the Derby. But it soon became known that the arrangement with Williamson would stand for Epsom, so Piggott would have to look elsewhere.

Look elsewhere is exactly what Piggott did – and quite extensively. Since he turned freelance in 1966, Piggott has done plenty of his jockeying for position *before* big races; getting on the right horse is often more than half the battle. But never has his name been linked with so many different partners in a big race as it was in connection with the 1972 Derby. At first it was taken for granted that he would ride Crowned Prince; when he fell by the wayside, a string of successors were found, including Moulton, Pentland Firth, Hard to Beat, Roberto, Our Mirage, Gombos, Ballymore, and Boucher. One by one, and for various reasons, they all dropped out of the calculations; then, on May 29 – two days after Williamson's injury – it was announced that Piggott's Derby mount was settled. He would ride Manitoulin, a stable companion of Roberto who had won recently at The Curragh, but whose form seemed distinctly inferior to that already shown by many of his prospective Epsom rivals. Rarely had a champion jockey been engaged for such a forlorn hope in the Derby.

However, that was by no means the end of the matter. At the weekend Roberto's owner, John Galbreath, arrived from America to see the colt he had bred carry his colours in the Derby. Not unnaturally, he was more than a little perturbed to hear that there was some doubt about the fitness of his jockey. It was an expensive enough operation to breed and rear a colt like Roberto. A lot of money went into the running of Galbreath's Darby Dan Farm in Kentucky, where he had been bred, and a lot more had been expended in shipping him halfway across the world to Vincent O'Brien, where he was treated to the best and probably the costliest training available. Roberto was shaping up for the most important day of his life, and there was a question mark over the fitness of the man on top! All that planning, all that expense could go to waste in the last two and a half minutes of the operation, when the difference between winning and losing might be measured at as much as $3,000,000. The prize money was only a fraction of that, but the prestige of victory would add fortunes to his value as a stallion.

Galbreath's course was clear. The way he saw it, Williamson could not be risked on Roberto. Piggott was already booked to ride Mrs Galbreath's colt Manitoulin, so *that* switch could be effected without much bother. It was certainly hard luck on Williamson, whom he would have been perfectly happy to employ if there had not been that nagging doubt, and he proposed compensating the Australian by offering him the same percentage as Piggott in the event of success. Williamson might be running out of opportunities at 49, but Galbreath could hardly hope for many more at 75!

There is no doubt that Galbreath regarded his actions as not only justifiable, but inevitable. And they could also be construed as sporting, for they *guaranteed* a wonderful run for the thousands of pounds of public money which depended on Roberto's performance, and they made generous provision for the deposed jockey.

The trouble was that British and American ideas of what constitutes a 'sportsman' do not coincide. The home version was well illustrated a fortnight after the Derby, when John and Jean Hislop allowed Joe Mercer to ride the unbeaten Brigadier Gerard in the Prince of Wales's Stakes at Royal Ascot although he was clearly showing the mental and physical effects of being involved in an air crash less than forty-eight hours before. The attitude of those owners was inevitably contrasted favourably with Galbreath's. The American would have regarded their decision as the height of folly, even after Brigadier Gerard had run and won.

Galbreath was a different kind of sportsman. He had two passions, horses and baseball, and he was delighted to throw

94

fortunes into them. But he was also a businessman, and he wanted to see some return for his outlay. His grandfather had been a Methodist minister, his father an Ohio farmer. Galbreath himself went into business, establishing in 1925 a small construction firm which expanded and prospered famously until it ranked among the giants of US industry. In addition, Galbreath had become the chief shareholder in the Firestone Tyre Company as the result of his marriage. So when he branched out into racing and baseball, he was bound to follow his business instincts. He did not just support the Pittsburgh Pirates, or become one of their directors. He bought them. As far as racing was concerned, he purchased the 1955 Kentucky Derby winner, Swaps, for $2,000,000 and it was his almighty dollar which lured Ribot and Sea-Bird, the two greatest European throughbreds, on extended leases for stud duty in America. That was *his* idea of being a sportsman. To European eyes, perhaps the closest he ever came to displaying a sporting bent was when he named Roberto after his star player in the Pittsburgh Pirates, Roberto Clemente.

There, then, was Galbreath's view. He owned Roberto and he had an inalienable right to employ whomsoever he wished to ride his horses. In this case he wanted Piggott, and he told him so. The English champion could have refused, and many considered that he should have done so. But why should he? If Crowned Prince had not flattered only to deceive earlier in the year, Roberto would have been his mount in any case. And if he declined Galbreath's offer, Williamson would never have been re-instated. Another jockey would have been engaged, almost certainly an American. No, Piggott was bound to accept.

However, from Williamson's standpoint, all these thoughts were purely academic. The issue was his fitness, and he *was* fit. Aside from any question of Galbreath's loyalty to him, the Australian had been intensely faithful to his employer and the public. He had systematically set about preparing himself for the Derby and two days before the race his doctor had given him the 'all clear' to resume riding. It was on that very day that O'Brien and Galbreath confronted Williamson and informed him that he would not be required, that Piggott would replace him, and that he would not lose financially by the switch. There was no room for argument; the decision had been taken.

Williamson was understandably shocked and indignant.

The insult to his professional pride was intensified by the news that Piggott would, in effect, be riding for *him*, earning *his* present. An owner might look on a Derby victory as something which added another nought to his horse's already six-figure valuation; for a jockey there was no amount of money which could compensate for losing the mount, particularly when that jockey had never won a Derby before. Piggott had five Derby winners up his sleeve already; one more would bring him level with the record holder, Jem Robinson, whose six successes were gained between 1824 and 1836.

The Press and the public were with Williamson almost to a man. Roberto was most people's idea of the winner, but there was no doubt that he would have been an immensely popular loser in the circumstances.

After all the controversial preliminaries, nobody would have been the least bit surprised if the race itself had proved tame by comparison. It was never that. Roberto had the worst draw, number one in a field of 22, which meant that he had to start quickly or risk being cut off by a wall of horses when the course veers to the right on the uphill section. Piggott gave him just the start he needed, bouncing him out of the stalls and finding him a trouble-free spot near the rails after a couple of furlongs. Pentland Firth, with the up-and-coming star Pat Eddery in the saddle, forced a commendable pace which had a few runners in difficulties before halfway. As these poorer contestants dropped back, two fancied runners, Steel Pulse and the French colt Lyphard, were among those hampered.

On the descent to Tattenham Corner, Pentland Firth continued to lead, chased by Meadow Mint, Ormindo, Manitoulin, Palladium, and Mercia Boy. Roberto was handily placed in the following group, with Rheingold on his outside. In the course of the next furlong the pattern of the race took shape, with Pentland Firth galloping on strongly on the rails, pursued now by Roberto and Rheingold, who emerged from the pack at almost the same moment.

With two furlongs to go, the battle was well and truly on, as Roberto and Rheingold drew up to Pentland Firth together, and for a moment the trio raced in line abreast. The long-time leader was now put under pressure and he reacted by veering ever so slightly to the right, away from the rails. Simultaneously Ernie Johnson felt Rheingold edge to his left, and Roberto, the meat in the sandwich, was forced into Pentland Firth.

96

The bump came at just the wrong moment for Pentland Firth. He was beginning to tire anyway and this collision completely knocked the stuffing out of him. Roberto, too, was shaken momentarily off balance, leaving Rheingold in front and the almost certain winner, but Piggott gathered his mount together as only he can, driving the American colt up to renew his challenge. Now, although the lead lay with Rheingold, one precious advantage lay with Roberto – the inside berth. While both horses were tired, Roberto was at least able to keep straight; Rheingold hung persistently to his left on the camber which slopes away towards the rails, so that Johnson needed all his strength to avoid a disastrous collision. He would have needed another pair of hands to ride his most forceful finish as well.

In fact the pair did brush several times, but each somehow maintained his impetus, battling on doggedly amid mounting excitement. For all his erratic steering, Rheingold kept his narrow lead, seeming always to have the edge on his rival for pace.

But now, inside the final furlong, Piggott made the race-winning decision. Roberto was not finding quite enough, and unless Rheingold weakened significantly in those dying moments, all would be lost. The time had come to test Roberto's courage to the full; the whip must now be brought to bear with maximum effect.

The text books say that you should always whip a horse left-handed up the Epsom straight. They also say that you should never attempt to hit a horse at each beat of his gallop, or you will make him shorten stride rather than lengthen it. Piggott ignored both precepts; text books do not allow for genius. This was a desperate measure, but a controlled desperation such as perhaps even Piggott had never displayed before.

A dozen times in that last furlong the whip cracked down on Roberto's hind quarters with all the ferocity which the right hand of Britain's strongest jockey could command. Yet at the same time the left hand kept his mount as straight as a die and his body maintained perfect rhythm. The colt's gameness was amazing, but in a sense inevitable. If he had been going to flinch, it would have happened after the first almighty clout, and victory would have been handed on a plate to Rheingold. But Piggott would not have taken no for an answer at that time. The first crack had barely hit its target when down came number two. An irresistible rhythm was suddenly instilled as Piggott wound Roberto up to a frantic tempo which could only last for seconds. The only thing which mattered was whether the timing had been right – whether Roberto would generate that vital extra spurt at the all-important point, opposite the judge's box. The issue was still in doubt when the judge came within talking distance, and then, in the final 20 yards, Roberto was dealt four more crashing blows which produced the hard-earned effect. Head stretched out, Roberto pipped Rheingold by a couple of inches right on the post.

This was a finish of four heroes – Rheingold, who must have won comfortably with the rails position and a level course, and Ernie Johnson, who all but pulled off a famous victory in the direst circumstances; Roberto, the gamest if not the classiest of Derby winners, and Lester Piggott, whose demonic riding over the last furlong matched if not excelled anything he had ever done in an unparalleled career.

Yet where was the public acclaim for Piggott's genius? Nobody who witnessed the race could deny that Roberto owed his victory to Piggott. It is beyond belief that *any* other rider could have snatched that Derby out of the fire. But the announcement of the photo-finish verdict was greeted without enthusiasm and the connections of the winner were given a reception so frigid that it was a positive embarrassment to impartial observers.

As far as the public were concerned, Galbreath was the villain of the piece, with O'Brien and Piggott as his henchmen. Not even the fact that this trio had just combined to produce one of the most magical moments in Turf history could erase the belief that they were 'bad sports'.

Thirty-five minutes later, the crowd gave more positive voice to their feelings when Williamson brought Captive Dream home a comfortable winner of the Woodcote Stakes, while Piggott finished third on the odds-on favourite. 'Weary Willie' was cheered to the echo, as he was again later in the day when he won on Capistrano, with Piggott once more on the beaten favourite.

The public's sympathy for Williamson was easy to understand, but this was really a case with right on both sides. And the bad sportsmanship, if such it was, of Roberto's connections was certainly no worse than that shown by the crowd after the Derby. Their own sporting instincts were sadly inconspicuous when they failed to recognize the supreme achievement of the world's master jockey.

Williamson had his great moment less than a month later when he rode Steel Pulse to victory in the Irish Sweeps Derby at The Curragh. Roberto, almost certainly suffering as the result of his Epsom exertions, finished no nearer than twelfth, with Johnny Roe in the saddle. Williamson was offered a reunion with Roberto two months later in the Benson & Hedges Gold Cup at York, but he declined as he had already promised to ride in a comparatively minor event in Belgium on the same day. Piggott had elected to partner Rheingold this time, and Roberto won with the Panamanian Braulio Baeza in the saddle.

In fact, Williamson never rode Roberto again. But he was re-united, a year later, with the cause of all the bother, The Broker. That came in a minor race back at Kempton Park, where the story had begun. The pair came home in fifth place and never looked like getting any nearer. Look up the index to the form book and you will find that the next entry under The Broker's name reads simply 'dead'. But don't infer too much from that fact. Williamson was not that kind of rider, although some people would not have blamed him in the circumstances.

DERBY STAKES. At Epsom, Wednesday, 7 June 1972. 1½ miles. £63,735 to the winner. For 3-year-olds only.

J. W. Galbreath's b.c. Roberto, 9st 0lb	L. Piggott	1
H. R. K. Zeisel's b.c. Rheingold. 9st 0lb	E. Johnson	2
V. W. Hardy's b.c. Pentland Firth. 9st 0lb	P. Eddery	3
N. Cohen's ch.c. Our Mirage. 9st 0lb	F. Durr	4
J. R. Mullion's b.c. Gombos. 9st 0lb	C. Roche	5
A. J. Struthers's bl.c. Scottish Rifle. 9st 0lb	R. Hutchinson	6
G. A. Oldham's b.c. Ormindo. 9st 0lb	B. Taylor	7
R. N. Tikkoo's br.c. Steel Pulse. 9st 0lb	W. Pyers	8
R. B. Moller's b.c. Moulton. 9st 0lb	E. Hide	9
R. N. Webster's br.c. Meadow Mint. 9st 0lb	W. Carson	10
Mrs J. W. Galbreath's b.c. Manitoulin. 9st 0lb	W. Swinburn	11
Lady Z. Wernher's gr.c. Charling. 9st 0lb	J. Lindley	12
D. Wildenstein's b.c. Sukawa. 9st 0lb	Y. Saint-Martin	13
Countess M. Batthyany's b.c. Palladium. 9st 0lb	J. Higgins	14

Mme P. Wertheimer's b.c. Lyphard. 9st olb   F. Head 15
G. J. van der Ploeg's b.c. Mercia Boy. 9st olb   R. Marshall 16
Mrs V. Hue-Williams's ch.c. Yaroslav. 9st olb   G. Lewis 17
Lord Rosebery's b.c. Paper Cap. 9st olb   J. Gorton 18
Lady Beaverbrook's ch.c. Donello. 9st olb   J. Mercer 19
R. A. Woods's ch.c. Young Arthur. 9st olb   A. Murray 20
Mrs J. A. McDougald's b.c. Mezzanine. 9st olb   P. Waldron 21
Mme J. Couturié's br.c. Neptunium. 9st olb   A. Barclay 22

Winner bred by J. W. Galbreath. Trained by M. V. O'Brien.

Betting: 3–1 Roberto, 4–1 Lyphard, Yaroslav, 9–1 Steel
Pulse, 20–1 Ormindo, 22–1 Rheingold, Scottish Rifle, 28–1
Charling, 35–1 Neptunium, 40–1 Moulton, 50–1 Gombos,
Meadow Mint, Pentland Firth, 66–1 Sukawa, Manitoulin,
Palladium, 100–1 Our Mirage, 200–1 others.

Won by a short head, 3 lengths. Time: 2min 36.09sec.

RED RUM

*when a great Australian 'chaser treated Liverpool's fences
with contempt and forced a record feat from his conqueror*

We are often told that we inhabit a crazy world, so let's
believe it for a minute. Imagine that you have to frame the
conditions for a race which would be guaranteed to fail,
something that would attain the height of unpopularity with
all sections of the community.

You might start by choosing a location which the public
are known to dislike, where the amenities are antediluvian or
non-existent, and where it is impossible to see what is hap-
pening during most of the races. It would be best to make
your race a handicap, because in theory that should make all
the runners finish together, whereas in practice it generally
means that the best horse cannot win. Now limit your handicap
to a range of two stones, which will mean that the worst horses
are robbed of their chance, too. You should set the distance
of your race somewhat longer than any other race in the
calendar, so that all the horses will be unused to the journey,
they will all get exhausted and provide a most unedifying
spectacle. Now, the *coup de grâce*. Break up the journey
by placing thirty obstacles in their way – not the sort to which
they might be accustomed, but fences where the landing sides
are lower than the take-off sides. That will introduce danger
to life and limb. Excellent. You have scared away nearly all
the best horses. Now give a lot of prize money to attract
a plethora of bad horses and you should get wholesale
carnage.

That could even win our crazy contest; it sounds ghastly
enough. But it is, of course, the Grand National – or an only
slightly distorted version of what the Grand National might
be. Amazingly, this contest based on illogicalities and ab-
surdities maintains a firmer hold on the general public
than any other race, the Derby included. Thousands who
care nothing for horses or racing for 364 days of the year,
who would never dream of entering a betting shop or visiting

a racecourse, could not be parted from their television sets when the National is shown.

The reason is, basically, tradition. The Grand National has become an institution – part of the British way of life – and it retains its century-old glamour although the fences have been made easier and the best steeplechasers rarely contest it. Those facts cannot detract from its status as the most spectacular sporting event of the year – a source of perennial delight to millions of people, and something worth guarding jealously if only for that reason. The loss of Aintree racecourse, which has been 'imminent' since 1965, might not mean the death of the Grand National, for it would always be possible to stage a substitute elsewhere. But another venue, without a Becher's Brook, a Valentine's, a Canal Turn, or a Chair, could never sustain such an event as an institution. It would pass into a sort of limbo, along with the University Boat Race. Twenty years ago, half the country decorated themselves in light or dark blue favours and the media discoursed copiously on the prospects for weeks beforehand; now it seems that the crews meet in secret conclave and row for their own amusement.

Unlike the Boat Race, the Grand National has always provided superb entertainment as a spectacle. Yet it has frequently failed to delight the connoisseur. It would be idle to deny that there have been years when the cynic who defined it as 'a very long steeplechase' was nearer the truth than he intended. Slow horses over lengthy courses rate highly on my barometer of boredom. But the National has a habit of turning up memorable performances with a regularity no other jump race can match. And when that happens, Aintree, for all its dilapidated buildings and joke 'facilities', is the enthusiast's paradise. That was how it was on March 31 1973.

There were 38 contenders for the National on that chilly but dry afternoon, when the turf rode uncommonly firm. The betting suggested that the race would be dominated by three horses, the top weights Crisp and L'Escargot, and the improving lightweight Red Rum. And for once, the market proved an exceptionally accurate guide.

Crisp was Australian by birth and cosmopolitan by upbringing. A ten-year-old, he had been bred by his owner, Sir Chester Manifold, a one-time Cambridge University graduate with a long history of public service in Victoria government and in Victoria racing. Australia has never provided the most competitive steeplechasing in the world, but Crisp proved himself so much the best there – at least up to two and a half miles – that his owner felt confident enough about his ability to pit him against the best abroad. Accordingly, Sir Chester sent him first for the initial running of the Colonial Cup at Camden, South Carolina, then planned to ship him to England to join Fred Winter's string at Lambourn.

The Carolina venture failed in the strangest surroundings for a racecourse. The track itself, on Mrs Marion duPont Scott's private estate, was neatly laid out and the fences, more like over-sized English hurdles, were admirably constructed. But the highest point in the tiny public 'stand' was no more than 15 feet from terra firma, while the county laws forbade gambling and the sale of liquor – the two prerequisites for racing anywhere else. Perhaps because this was a gala occasion, when the USA was acting as host to five other nations, the police made no move to check either illegal enterprise. A couple of uniformed men watched me unconcerned as I struck my two dollar bet on Crisp and sank a Budweiser at the same time. I lost my money, for Crisp faded abruptly after making the running over the first twelve fences and came home seventh. The distance was more than two and three-quarter miles, so it seemed that the doubts about his stamina had been valid.

That was in November 1970. Crisp then flew to England and was given ample time to acclimatize to the rigours of a Lambourn Winter. His new handler did not subject him to the racecourse test until March 1971, when he was saddled for a modest handicap over two miles at Wincanton. He won handsomely by 15 lengths, carrying top weight of 12st 7lb, then, only five days later, he beat the best specialists at the distance in the Champion Two-Mile 'Chase at Cheltenham.

A year afterwards Crisp proved his class over three miles with a comfortable victory over doughty rivals like The Dikler, Kinloch Brae, and Titus Oates at Kempton Park. That performance was sufficient to make him favourite for the Cheltenham Gold Cup, but he faded in the closing stages of that three and a quarter mile championship and finished only fifth. Again it looked as though he had failed for want of staying power, but Fred Winter would not agree. Indeed, he resolved to prove his point by aiming Crisp at the Grand National in

1973, leading up to Aintree with four races at much shorter distances. He won one, at two and a half miles, then finished third in the Two-Mile Champion 'Chase, his final preliminary. Crisp had been allotted joint top weight of 12 stones in the National, but it was clear that he would prove a serious threat to one and all if he stayed the four and a half miles. Fred Winter maintained his faith in the gelding and he really ought to know, for he had ridden two National winners (Sundew and Kilmore) and had saddled two more (Anglo and Jay Trump).

Crisp shared the market leadership at 9–1 with Red Rum, an eight-year-old who had also come to the fore in a rather unconventional manner. He had been bred for flat racing – his sire ran second in the one mile 2000 Guineas and was himself a son of the sprinter Vilmorin – and he had been sold as a yearling for only 400 guineas to trainer Tim Molony, a former champion rider over jumps. On his first outing as a two-year-old, Red Rum dead-heated for first place in a selling plate at Aintree, two days before the 1967 Grand National. Two more modest victories followed for Molony's stable before he was sold to go hurdling in the colours of Mrs Lurline Brotherton. Here was another Aintree connection, for it was she who owned the 1950 Grand National winner, Freebooter. Trained first by Bobby Renton, then by Tommy Stack and Tony Gillam, Red Rum won three hurdle races and five steeplechases, but never gave any indication that he might emulate Freebooter. Most people surmised that he had passed his peak when Mrs Brotherton sent him to the Doncaster Sales in August 1972. One man, though, thought differently and he had a commission to buy a Grand National prospect if he could find one to suit. Red Rum suited him fine and he got the gelding for 6000 guineas.

The buyer was Donald 'Ginger' McCain, a motor dealer from Southport who dabbled a bit in training – his lifetime tally of winners was three – from unpretentious stables at the back of his somewhat grander car showrooms. His client was 84-year-old Noel Le Mare, who came from the same Lancashire resort and who had cherished an ambition to own a Grand National winner ever since he saw Eremon win the great 'chase back in 1907.

Red Rum took on a fresh lease of life in his new surroundings, winning his first five races for the stable in the space of six weeks. He ran three more times without winning before he came to Aintree, but his most recent form, when fourth to Tregarron at Haydock Park, indicated that he must pose a real threat with only 10st 5lb in the saddle.

L'Escargot, like Crisp, was set to carry 12 stones in the National, and he was another much-travelled competitor with a string of important successes to his credit. Bred and trained in Ireland, but owned by the American Raymond Guest, he had been a top-class hurdler, and as long ago as 1969 was voted 'Jumper of the Year' in the USA following two outings at New York's Belmont Park track, where he won the Meadow Brook 'Chase and ran third in the Temple Gwathmey 'Chase. He had conquered the best steeplechasers in the British Isles when landing the Cheltenham Gold Cups of 1970 and 1971, returning to the States in between to run fourth in the Colonial Cup, in front of Crisp. In his most recent start before this, his first Aintree bid, L'Escargot had finished fourth in the 1973 Cheltenham Gold Cup, which was run in record time. He was, and was to remain for some time yet, a formidable contender in the best company. His two Gold Cup victories made him arguably the class horse of the race so that he was naturally a popular third favourite at 11–1.

Crisp, Red Rum, and L'Escargot were but three of the 38 contestants for the richest prize in National Hunt racing, yet the conditions – a firm surface, guaranteeing a true gallop throughout – suggested that this trio of class horses ought to dispute the £25,486 first prize. The indifferent runners should be left behind, or could be expected to get in each other's way and drop out of contention. It was up to the riders of the big three to keep their mounts out of trouble – not always the easiest task at Aintree.

The tension before the start of the Grand National is hard enough for the average spectator to bear, but for the jockeys with the awesome responsibility of guiding the nation's cash in the biggest betting race of the year it is like nothing on earth. There is an hour and a quarter between the first race on the card, a hurdles event, and the big 'chase. Those who ride in the opener may hope to forget about the National for a few minutes, but they are generally too concerned about avoiding injury to concentrate on their job. Some without a mount in the hurdle may risk a drop or two of Dutch courage, if they have no weight problems, while others have been known to lock themselves in the lavatory for an hour or so.

The tedious parade and the roll-call down at the start

intensify the torment, allowing the student of human nature one of the sights of the year. Never, outside a mental institution, will he see a more numerous collection of lunatics in one place. For, make no mistake, these fellows need a streak of lunacy to subject themselves to this body-breaking, mind-bending terror for six days a week. Here, moments before the most agonizing nerve-stretcher of all races, many experience the only brief seconds of lucidity they will know in a season. For weeks they have yearned to know (or know again) the thrill of competing in the most famous steeplechase in the world. Now, when their sense of exhilaration should be mounting to its peak, they wonder why on earth they came into this game in the first place and wish that it was all over. There is always a fair amount of banter at the start, with the extroverts displaying their nerves in the feeblest attempts at humour, while the introverts betray their condition with a weak smile or a preoccupied glance in the opposite direction. If you are on a fancied horse, you worry. If you are on a dodgy jumper, you worry. Only those on no-hopers with proven jumping ability can actually look forward to enjoying their ride. At least they can take their time and treat it like a good day's hunting; and, who knows, perhaps some of those up front will fall and then anything might happen – that was how John Buckingham won on Foinavon.

On this occasion, the riders of the big three seemed less affected than the others – after all, they were all entitled to a measure of confidence. Crisp's rider Richard Pitman had enjoyed a marvellously successful season, apart from his short-head defeat with Pendil in the Cheltenham Gold Cup, and he knew he had a safe conveyance. Brian Fletcher, on Red Rum, had a mount who had never fallen in his life, and he had the memory of a winning ride on Red Alligator in the 1968 National to lift him. Tommy Carberry had won two Gold Cups on L'Escargot, and he was Irish; it always helps to be Irish in the horse business, especially when the pressure is on.

As the line formed for the cavalry charge towards the first fence, these seemed to be the great triumvirate. They would prove it, too, but not until their numbers were hoisted into the frame would spectators think of them as a threesome again. Indeed, from the moment they left the gate until they stood side by side in the unsaddling enclosure they never once figured in the same field of vision.

The confirmed front-runner Grey Sombrero, hero of the 1972 Whitbread Gold Cup, set a strong gallop on the straight section running away from the stands, and Pitman sent Crisp along to keep him company. Fletcher kept Red Rum in mid-division, while Carberry was content to remain 'lost' among the stragglers in these early stages. Grey Sombrero held a narrow advantage over the first five fences, but at Becher's, the sixth, Crisp swept by with a prodigious leap and set off for the Canal Turn as the clear leader. He was to cover three and a half more miles before he saw another horse.

After rounding the Canal Turn, the field made their way back towards the stands, taking six more fences *en route*. Throughout that section Crisp jumped superbly, extending his lead all the time, yet with astonishing economy of effort. He was burning up the turf, but met every obstacle in his stride and cleared them as though they did not exist. Aintree had seen many tearaway front-runners before, but none who jumped so fluently. Horses of this disposition are generally erratic at their fences, scaring jockey and public alike; Crisp drew only gasps of admiration from the crowd as he leaped faultlessly, drew away smoothly on landing, and continued to widen his advantage on the flat.

Crisp crossed the two fences in front of the stands in impeccable style, the mighty Chair and the long, low water jump finding him as adaptable as he was fluent. His margin had now stretched to twenty lengths, with the 100–1 shot Endless Folly nearest to him after Grey Sombrero had crashed with a broken shoulder at the Chair. As Pitman steered Crisp to the left to start his second circuit there were still 24 runners in pursuit, and it was noticeable that Red Rum had advanced to fifth spot, going strongly and jumping well. L'Escargot still had a lot to do if he was to take a hand in the finish, for he had sixteen in front of him. He would need the proverbial luck of the Irish to avoid interference.

There was no slackening of Crisp's pace as he strode majestically away from the stands, still meeting every fence with the same immaculate precision and gaining ground in the air. He had already run nearly all his rivals off their legs and there was still no challenger within hail.

It was at this point that Brian Fletcher decided to take action. He had thought it inconceivable that Crisp would sustain his blistering gallop throughout, but now he could no longer afford to pin his hopes to a possible and so far invisible chink in the leader's armour. A more positive approach had to be taken before it was too late, and Crisp himself had become invisible. After the eighteenth fence had been negotiated Red Rum was given the message and, as Endless Folly weakened, the locally trained champion assumed second place at the next. By the time he reached Becher's for the second time, Red Rum had left all his pursuers adrift, perhaps fifteen lengths or more, yet for all his increase in tempo he had made no inroads into Crisp's massive advantage. *He* was now nearly a fence in front, still running away and hiding!

Around the Canal Turn, over Valentine's and back towards the stands, Crisp maintained his furious gallop, skipping over those formidable fences as though they were hurdles and promising to pursue his solo career until the end. After the twenty-eighth fence, Crisp still had some twenty lengths in hand and there seemed no future for Red Rum. He had chased the leader gamely for the best part of two miles, but now it seemed that he, like all the others, would be run into the ground.

Fletcher, though, would not give up. He kept pushing away, hoping and praying that something might yet happen to swing the advantage his way. With such a willing mount as Red Rum, still battling on courageously in pursuit of a target he could barely see, Fletcher owed it to him to try.

Then it happened. Between the last two fences, with Crisp still fifteen lengths up, Richard Pitman glanced over his shoulder. Fletcher read this unintentioned signal aright. Crisp was tiring and his jockey was anxious to know the position of his nearest rival. There *was* a chink in that armour and the faint chance existed that it still might be exposed!

Fletcher redoubled his efforts, Red Rum answered his urgent calls valiantly, and even though the deficit at the last fence was still more than ten lengths, it was clear from the stands that there might yet be a race. The issue had seemed cut and dried for the last three miles; now it was back in the balance with the run-in of 494 yards to be covered – a gruelling finale to the severest steeplechase course in the country.

Pitman had sat as still as possible throughout the contest – the only possible course of action on a horse with suspect stamina – but he could sit still no longer. His rival was gaining ground and he *had* to ask Crisp for a renewed effort. After all the wonders he had performed, another at this stage would have been a miracle, and it was not forthcoming. Pitman went for his whip and Crisp's effort collapsed as suddenly as if he had been pole-axed.

With no rail on his inside to guide him, Crisp floundered like a drunken man, veering to the left and almost running out as he came to the 'elbow' in the final furlong. He still had the lead, but Red Rum had the bit between his teeth now and was bearing down inexorably on the outside. He had an advantage of 23lb in the weights and it was telling with every stride.

There was nothing that Pitman or Crisp could do now. Thousands in the stands, including many of Red Rum's backers, willed the Australian horse to stay in front for those final few strides, but, for the umpteenth time at Aintree, justice was seen not to be done. Red Rum flashed past in the last ten yards to take the verdict by three-quarters of a length. No fewer than 25 lengths farther back, L'Escargot plodded home third, having run through a string of horses on the second circuit.

Everybody knew that they had witnessed a magnificent performance, but not until the time was announced did they fully appreciate its excellence. Red Rum had covered the distance (or rather Crisp had made him cover the distance) in 9 minutes 1.9 seconds – no less than 18.5 seconds faster than the record set by Golden Miller in 1934.

Poor Crisp, assuredly the hero, if not the winner, of that Grand National, was never one of fortune's favourites. He positively trounced Red Rum when they met again at level weights over three and a quarter miles at Doncaster, but on that occasion the winner's prize was £1763 instead of £25,486. What is more, Crisp injured himself so badly in the course of that race that he could not run again during the 1973–74 season. That ill-luck was underlined in the most emphatic manner when Red Rum took advantage of Crisp's absence to notch his second National win, and this time *he* carried top weight of 12 stones.

Even L'Escargot's Grand National turn came in 1975, when he turned the tables on Red Rum thanks to a substantial turnover in the weights. So, of the 'great triumvirate' of 1973, only Crisp, demonstrably the greatest Aintree jumper of the post-war era, failed to secure his due reward.

Rough justice, perhaps, but there is something more to the Grand National than the winner's 'pot'; the result is un-important, compared with the race itself. Red Rum really needed his 1974 victory to ensure his place in history. Without it, he would have become steeplechasing's counterpart to marathon running's Johnny Hayes and Jim McGhee. Nobody remembers them these days, while the names of the 'moral winners' they beat, Dorando Pietri and Jim Peters, are immortal. The 1973 Grand National, unquestionably, belonged to Crisp.

GRAND NATIONAL STEEPLECHASE (Handicap). At Aintree, Saturday, 31 March 1973. 4 miles 856 yards. £25,486 to the winner. For 6-year-olds and up.

N. H. Le Mare's b.g. Red Rum. 8yrs, 10st 5lb B. Fletcher		1
Sir C. Manifold's br.g. Crisp. 10yrs, 12st 0lb R. Pitman		2
R. R. Guest's ch.g. L'Escargot. 10yrs, 12st 0lb T. Carberry		3
E. R. Courage's b.g. Spanish Steps. 10yrs, 11st 13lb P. Blacker		4
B. P. Jenks's b.g. Rouge Autumn. 9yrs, 10st 0lb K. B. White		5
D. J. Proctor's b.g. Hurricane Rock. 9yrs, 10st 0lb R. Champion		6
Sir J. Thomson's br.g. Proud Tarquin. 10yrs, 10st 11lb Lord Oaksey		7
Mrs C. M. Richards's ch.g. Prophecy. 10yrs, 10st 3lb B. R. Davies		8
Mrs V. Vanden Bergh's br.g. Endless Folly. 11yrs, 10st 0lb J. Guest		9
Mrs J. Watney's b.g. Black Secret. 9yrs, 11st 2lb S. Barker		10
P. Blackburn's b.g. Petruchio's Son. 10yrs, 10st 5lb D. Mould		11
Mrs J. Bowes-Lyon's br.g. The Pooka. 11yrs, 10st 0lb A. Moore		12
J. Rowles's b.g. Great Noise. 9yrs, 10st 2lb D. Cartwright		13
A. M. Darlington's ch.g. Green Plover. 13yrs, 10st 0lb Mr M. Morris		14
Mrs R. E. Sangster's ch.g. Sunny Lad. 9yrs, 10st 3lb W. Smith		15
Mrs H. O'Neill's b.g. Go-Pontinental. 13yrs, 10st 4lb J. McNaught		16
E. F. Birchall's ch.g. Mill Door. 11yrs, 10st 5lb P. Cullis		17
W. F. Caudwell's gr.g. Grey Sombrero. 9yrs, 10st 9lb W. Shoemark, fell		

N. H. Le Mare's b.g. Glenkiln. 10yrs, 10st 7lb

J. J. O'Neill, fell

Mrs D. W. Samuel's br.g. Beggar's Way. 9yrs, 10st 1lb

T. Kinane, fell

R. R. Guest's b.g. Ashville. 8yrs, 10st 4lb J. King, fell

Mrs J. H. Weekes's br.g. Tarquin Bid. 9yrs, 10st 0lb

J. Bracken, fell

Mrs E. J. Taplin's b.g. Richeleau. 9yrs, 10st 0lb

N. Kernick, fell

L. G. Scott's b.g. Charley Winking. 8yrs, 10st 0lb

Mr D. Scott, fell

R. F. Fisher's b.g. Proud Percy. 10yrs, 10st 0lb

R. R. Evans, fell

B. J. Brookes's ch.g. Culla Hill, 9yrs, 10st 7lb

Mr N. Brookes, fell

Lord Zetland's br.g. Canharis, 8yrs, 10st 1lb

P. Buckley, brought down

G. Sloan's b.g. Fortune Bay. 9yrs, 10st 3lb

Owner, rider unseated

C. Freestone's b.g. Swan-Shot. 10yrs, 10st 0lb

M. Blackshaw, refused

Mrs E. Newman's ch.g. General Symons. 10yrs, 10st 0lb

P. Kiely, pulled up

Mrs J. Dening's b.g. Highland Seal. 10yrs, 10st 6lb

D. Nicholson, pulled up

Mrs F. Harvey's b.g. Mr Vimy. 10yrs, 10st 2lb

J. Haine, pulled up

B. P. Jenks's ch.g. Astbury. 10yrs, 10st 0lb

J. Bourke, pulled up

D. Ancil's b.g. Beau Parc. 10yrs, 10st 1lb

A. Turnell, pulled up

C. H. Nathan's b.g. Rough Silk. 10yrs, 10st 0lb

T. Norman, pulled up

J. E. Bigg's b.m. Princess Camilla. 8yrs, 10st 4lb

R. Barry, pulled up

J. Rose's br.g. Rampsman, 9yrs, 10st 0lb D. Munro, pulled up

Duke of Alburquerque's b.g. Nereo. 7yrs, 10st 3lb

Owner, pulled up

Winner bred by M. J. McEnery. Trained by D. McCain.

Betting: 9–1 Crisp, Red Rum, 11–1 L'Escargot, 14–1
Ashville, 16–1 Princess Camilla, Spanish Steps, Canharis,

20–1 Prophecy, Highland Seal, 22–1 Proud Tarquin, Black Secret, 25–1 Sunny Lad, Grey Sombrero, 33–1 Beggar's Way, General Symons, Glenkiln, 40–1 Rouge Autumn, 50–1 Astbury, Great Noise, Petruchio's Son, Richeleau, 66–1 Nereo, Fortune Bay, Rough Silk, 100–1 others.

Won by $\frac{3}{4}$ length, 25 lengths. Time: 9min 01.9sec.

BELMONT STAKES, BELMONT PARK, USA, JUNE 9 1973

SECRETARIAT

when the first American Triple Crown winner for 25 years shattered records galore

It is hard enough, in all conscience, to solve the multifarious mysteries of the Turf on a day-to-day basis, analysing the form and assessing the merits of the competitors to anything like a reasonable degree of accuracy. Opinions tend to become costly, and the only certain way to end up with a small fortune in racing is to start with a big one.

But the ultimate riddle of the Turf costs nothing at all and is even more fascinating for the fact that it *cannot* be solved. It exists only in the imagination. . . .

The scene is the racecourse in the Elysian Fields, and the going, naturally, is perfect. The twenty greatest thoroughbreds of all time are lined up at the start of the ultimate horse race. The universally accepted classic distance of a mile and a half has to be covered and every runner is at the peak of his or her powers. The weights have been adjusted to allow for the different stages of their development. Training and jockeyship, as is only to be expected in paradise, are sublime. Indeed, all the relevant factors are equal. Heaven knows no mishaps or infringements. It is a straight test of merit.

Of course, only the heavenly handicapper, with two centuries of world-wide form at his finger-tips, would be able to determine the composition of the field. Only he would have the answers to all the multitude of questions which arise from the problem. But mere mortals may conjure up their own visions of the competitors, applying earthly standards like times, winning margins, weights carried and the quality of the fields they beat. No two people would ever compile the same list of runners; few would come close to verity.

But there are a select few who *must* be there – horses who dominated other top-class competitors consistently and who, at least once in their lives, achieved a standard of excellence which forced the wisest and most experienced judges to admit that, on that day, it was inconceivable that any horse ever foaled could have done better.

Secretariat, then, must be there. His overall record may fall short of the traditional notion of a paragon, for unlike Kincsem, St Simon, Ormonde, Ribot, and many other notable performers, he was not unbeaten. He had the occasional off day. But when Secretariat applied all the locomotive power his generous frame *could* develop, there was no racehorse capable of living with him.

The Secretariat saga began with Christopher Chenery, a self-made millionaire from Virginia who established Meadow Stud at Doswell, 20 miles north of the state capital, Richmond. That was in the years immediately before World War II. By 1950, Meadow Stud had a classic winner to its credit (Hill Prince in the Preakness Stakes) and Chenery had made the most judicious purchase of his life by giving $30,000 for the mare Imperatrice. She was to throw ten winners and one filly who did not win a cent herself, but was to breed the winners of over $2,000,000, among them Secretariat.

Chenery built up an excellent band of broodmares over the years and he patronized the best stallions to give them the best chances. He was particularly keen on Bold Ruler, eight times the champion US sire, but somewhat less enthusiastic about forking out what he regarded as the exorbitant stud fee for the stallion's services. To get over this knotty problem, Chenery made a rather eccentric bargain with Bold Ruler's owner, Ogden Phipps. Each year he would send two of his choicely bred mares to the horse and the two men would toss a coin to determine the ownership of the foals, the winner taking first choice and the loser automatically getting that privilege in the following year.

This little ritual was enacted every two years, persisting even after the octogenarian Chenery's once agile brain had cracked and he had left Meadow permanently for hospital. His daughter, Mrs Penny Tweedy, took over the management of the stud, so it was she who attended for the biennial reunion in the autumn of 1969, when the futures of a colt out of Hasty Matelda and a filly out of Somethingroyal, plus an unborn foal in the latter mare were decided. The same two mares had been covered by Bold Ruler that spring, but only Somethingroyal was pregnant, so it would be 'Hobson's Choice' next year for the 1969 loser and nothing to come for the winner. In the circumstances, neither would have minded losing.

The coin was spun by Alfred Vanderbilt in his office at Belmont Park racecourse and Phipps called 'Tails!' The noted breeder 'Bull' Hancock, there to witness this strange contract, retrieved the 50 cent piece from the floor and reported, 'Tails it is!' Phipps had won the toss and made the biggest mistake of his life. Neither of the 1969 foals was of any use for racing purposes. Phipps took the filly, The Bride, who never got nearer than sixth in only four outings, while Mrs Tweedy's colt, Rising River, ran only once and earned nothing. But Mrs Tweedy was left with the foal inside Somethingroyal who came along just after midnight on March 30 1970 – and that was Secretariat.

Penny Tweedy lived in New York – she had the Meadow's racing stable to manage as well as the stud – so she was not on hand when the gangling chesnut with three white 'stockings' made his entry into the world. But she saw him soon afterwards and was so profoundly impressed that she was lost for words. While all the other foals on the farm were given graphic descriptions, Secretariat inspired just a single expletive in Mrs Tweedy's notebook – 'Wow!'

The colt's superb physique was apparent even at this early stage and he was to develop in proportion, evoking similar gasps of admiration from all who saw him – standing still, not racing! The late Charlie Hatton, greatest of all Turf writers, lyricised, 'Trying to fault Secretariat's conformation is like dreaming of dry rain.' Pimlico racetrack official Chick Lang mused, 'It's as though God wanted to create one perfect racehorse.' He was indeed a model thoroughbred, his symmetry aesthetically delightful, his strength awesome to contemplate, and his temperament ideally relaxed. And what is more, he could run. With a rear end reminiscent of a Sherman tank, he could generate phenomenal propulsion; with his massive stride, 25 feet at a full gallop, he could see off any challenge; with his immaculate conformation, he could co-ordinate his talents and adapt them to any conditions; with his vast heart (medical tests have estimated its weight at between 14 and 17 pounds, even larger than Phar Lap's), he could outstay the stoutest rival.

The fact of Secretariat's superior conformation and physique set him apart from other horses off the track as much as on it. But it was naturally his use of those assets on the racecourse, in competition with the next best horses around, which established his charisma. At the height of his fame,

Mrs Tweedy had to engage three full-time secretaries to handle his fan mail – up to 200 letters a day. She also had to hire an agency, the one which also looked after Katherine Hepburn, Elvis Presley, Jack Lemmon, and Sophia Loren, to exercise some form of control on the use of his name for commercial purposes. A Las Vegas night club offered $15,000 a performance for him just to walk on stage. His photograph adorned the front covers of those august magazines *Time* and *Newsweek*. And the noted columnist Art Buchwald opined that President Nixon would be wise to co-opt Secretariat to the White House staff, because he at least was universally respected.

That was what Secretariat accomplished. The way he did it was with a series of spectacular performances in a meteoric career lasting less than sixteen months. The bare figures show that he had 21 races, of which he won 16, was second in three, third once and fourth once; his total earnings came to $1,316,808.

Secretariat had his introduction to racing on Independence Day, 1972, but it was no gala occasion for the imposing ruddy hued youngster with the tall reputation. Indeed, a colt inbued with less character could have been soured for his racing life by the unfortunate experience suffered by Secretariat immediately after the stalls opened for that maiden purse at Aqueduct. A modest individual called Quebec caused the bother by ducking sharply to his left. The upshot of this unintentional manoeuvre was that Secretariat, running along the inside rail, received a severe buffeting. It would have been hard to imagine a worse beginning for a big and inexperienced colt. Thrown off balance and driven out of contention, he had his strength to thank for the aversion of complete disaster The distance of the race was only five and a half furlongs, so there was no possibility of his recovering all the lost ground. Yet his dour fighting qualities advanced him eight lengths and six places in the final straight, so that he finished fourth (the worst placing of his career) only a length and a quarter behind the winner.

It was clear that Secretariat would prove the top-class horse he had always looked. Meadow Stable had just won the Kentucky Derby and the Preakness Stakes with a very good colt called Riva Ridge, yet trainer Lucien Laurin, a French-Canadian with long experience of handling high-grade performers, had always insisted that this was a colt of far greater potential.

Secretariat bore out that opinion by finishing first in each of his next eight races that year, all in the space of four months. A maiden race at Aqueduct started the sequence, followed by an allowance event at Saratoga. Advancing into better company at the same track, he streaked to victory in the Sanford and Hopeful Stakes, then moved on to Belmont Park to capture the Futurity Stakes. Four weeks later he was tried at a mile for the first time in the Champagne Stakes, confounding the critics who had doubted his stamina by clearing an early 15-length deficit with an astonishing surge of power and flashing by to win by two lengths. However, although he was undoubtedly the best horse in the race, he was relegated to second place by the Stewards for brushing the runner-up, Stop the Music, during his electrifying dash.

The interference Secretariat caused was minimal, but the officials would have been failing in their duty if they had not upheld their own rules, so they reversed the placings of the first two. Nobody took their decision as a true reflection of the pair's relative merits, so that when they met again in the Laurel Futurity a fortnight later Secretariat was favourite at 1-10. Coming with his now familiar dash in the final straight, the big chesnut stormed clear without ever being asked to extend himself, and beat Stop the Music by eight lengths.

After two more weeks Secretariat completed his juvenile campaign with an equally facile victory in the Garden State Stakes to clinch the title of 'Best Two-Year-Old Colt'. Far more significantly, his extraordinary string of successes gained him the accolade of 'Horse of the Year', an honour never attained previously by one of his age group.

Secretariat rested on those laurels for over four months, demolishing a daily ration of 16 quarts of oats and continuing to fill out his already massive frame. His name was rarely out of the news, despite his temporary withdrawal from competition. The Press speculated freely on his prospects for the Triple Crown races – the Kentucky Derby, the Preakness, and Belmont Stakes – and at the end of February came the announcement of his syndication for a world record sum of $6,080,000. This move had been made necessary by the death, after six years' tragically debilitating illness, of Christopher Chenery. He had shown a flicker of recognition when his daughter appeared on television with Riva Ridge's Kentucky Derby trophy in her hands, but he expired on January 3 1973 without ever knowing of Secretariat's attainments. Only by syndicating Secretariat and Riva Ridge (whose price was $5,120,000) could taxes on the Chenery estate be settled. The 32 investors who bought into Secretariat at $190,000 a throw took a courageous risk, for history abounds with examples of two-year-old champions who failed to make the grade at three. But their gamble was gloriously vindicated, for by the end of the year it was reckoned that the terms could have been renegotiated at a valuation of $10,000,000. Indeed, as much as $500,000 was offered for a single share. The syndicate agreement concluded in February stipulated that Secretariat would continue to race in the name of Meadow Stable and that he would be retired from racing not later than November 15.

The champion was back in action at Aqueduct on March 17 for the Bay Shore Stakes, which he won easily by 4½ lengths. He needed that race badly, for his gluttonous appetite had brought his weight up to an incredibly burly 1555lb. Five races later, by the end of the Triple Crown series in June, he had reduced by over 400lb. In the Gotham Stakes he recorded another comfortable victory, equalling the track record as he did so, but a shock reverse came in the Wood Memorial Stakes, when he could finish no nearer than third behind his own stable companion, Angle Light.

The Wood Memorial was Secretariat's final preparatory race for the Kentucky Derby, so the classic programme opened amid a flurry of rumours and counter-rumours concerning the colt's fitness. His connections never lost faith in him, but some sections of the Press deserted him in favour of Sham, a big winner on the West Coast and runner-up in the Wood Memorial.

Secretariat silenced the doubters with an astounding display in the 99th running of America's greatest prestige event. As they passed the winning post on the first circuit jockey Ron Turcotte had him in last position, but as the race wore on 'Big Red' piled on the pressure in unprecedented fashion. Remorselessly stepping up his pace throughout the ten furlongs, Secretariat covered his first quarter mile in 25.2 seconds, his second in 24.2, his third in 23.6, his fourth in 23.4 and his fifth in 23.0. He had shaken off all bar Sham by the entry to the straight, then he proceeded to wear down that persistent challenger before the final furlong was reached. The victory margin was 2½ lengths and the time, 1 minute

59.4 seconds, smashed the record set by Northern Dancer (2 minutes exactly) nine years before.

The Preakness Stakes, which is run at nine and a half furlongs, was almost a precise replica of the Derby, for Secretariat secured the second jewel in the Triple Crown by the same margin over Sham, but this time was 0.4 seconds off the track record set by Cañonero in the 1971 classic.

There had been eight previous winners of the Triple Crown to show that the feat was possible, but in recent ultra-competitive times people began to wonder whether it would ever be achieved again. Since Citation captured all three legs in 1948, no fewer than six colts (Tim Tam, Carry Back, Northern Dancer, Kauai King, Majestic Prince, and Cañonero) had annexed the first two classics but failed as hot favourites in the mile and a half Belmont Stakes. All had come up against better stayers in this, the most testing of the three events, and many people now cast dubious glances at Secretariat's pedigree and proclaimed that his sire, Bold Ruler, had so far failed to sire any important winners over so long a journey.

However, Secretariat was something more than his pedigree. He was a physical specimen quite uncharacteristic of his sire and from the way he had been running recently there was no reason to doubt that a mile and a half would be within his compass. Furthermore, if he was to be beaten, who would deliver the crushing blow? He had only four rivals – three nonentities and Sham, a most courageous colt but one who had been clearly outpointed by the champion in two earlier rounds.

No, the public was convinced that Secretariat would win and they gave him their moral support at odds of 1–10. The only query, so far as they were concerned, was by how far he would win. None would have guessed that in a month of Sundays.

There were 67,605 spectators present at Belmont Park on that fine June afternoon, but there was a multi-million audience for the eighth race on the card, with an estimated 60 per cent of the nation's television sets turned to Secretariat's bid for the Triple Crown. The act at the top of the bill rose to the occasion as a star performer should, displaying talents of the highest order and dispensing them with elements of surprise, panache, and sheer excitement.

The surprise came from the word go. Ever since that terrifying introduction at Aqueduct eleven months before, Secretariat had always started slowly, taking a while to find his immaculate rhythm, then shifting into top gear in the closing stages to pulverize his opponents for speed. This time it was different. When the stalls opened, 'Big Red' flew out as though the hounds of Hell were at his heels, slipping instantly into a gear that would 'lose' all but the highest grade sprinters.

Laffit Pincay, on Sham, was not prepared for this tactic. He had expected to make the running, intent on testing Secretariat's suspect stamina, as he knew that Sham could never match his rival for finishing speed. Pincay, the most gifted rider in the USA, had to counter Turcotte's move and give immediate chase. The other runners were forgotten as Sham was bustled up to get in contention.

After two furlongs the scampering Sham had almost succeeded. Secretariat led him by no more than a head and, if he could not get past, at least he was pushing his opponent all the way. For the next quarter mile the furious duel continued, with Secretariat preserving his narrow advantage. A glance at the clock showed that they had covered the first half-mile in 46.2 seconds, a pace which seemed suicidal in a twelve-furlong classic. At this rate they would surely kill each other off and leave the race at the mercy of the pursuing group. Triple Crown aspirations would die for another year.

It did not work out like that. The pair continued to roar away down the back straight, ten lengths clear of the third horse, My Gallant, and there was no slackening of the pace. Then, as they came to the halfway point, this heady confrontation came to a sudden halt. Sham was beaten. He had given his all, may even have inched ahead of Secretariat once or twice, but he simply could not keep countering the superhorse's attacks. As Sham's heroic effort flattened, Secretariat opened a length's advantage. In seconds it was five lengths; at the end of a mile, reached in near-record time of 1 minute 34.2 seconds, it was seven lengths back to Sham and seven more to My Gallant.

It scarcely seemed possible that the lead could widen further. If Secretariat had the limitations of staying power his pedigree suggested, he would soon begin to tire himself. Besides which, he now lacked the spur of competition to drive him on and he could well develop a tendency to idle.

Neither eventuality occurred and, incredibly, Secretariat

actually increased the tempo in the fifth quarter mile. Stretching out in magnificent style, he drew further and further away from his rivals, who were now switching positions between themselves but with supreme irrelevance to the destiny of first prize. Secretariat passed the mile and quarter mark in 1 minute 59 seconds, a full second faster than the track record Kelso had tied in the 1961 Woodward Stakes and 0.4 seconds brisker than his own Kentucky Derby time. He was now twenty lengths clear of Twice a Prince, who had a head to spare over My Gallant.

By the final turn the margin had been extended to 28 lengths and here Secretariat found another rival. There was no horse in sight, but the electronic timepiece on the infield tote board *was* coming into view. Ron Turcotte knew that the track record had stood to Gallant Man at 2 minutes 26.6 seconds since the 1958 Belmont Stakes; he knew that he was on schedule to lower it; and he knew that Secretariat still had more to give.

Turcotte now asked for that final thrust and Secretariat delivered. The big colt's enthusiasm for the task was astounding. He was bred to run and he was loving every moment of it. Stretching his elegant head, which was somewhat less elegantly shrouded in a pair of blue and white checked blinkers, Secretariat sustained his charge all the way to the line and far beyond in his solo *tour de force*.

Turcotte's triumph was complete as they reached the post in 2 minutes 24 seconds, fragmenting Gallant Man's track record by 2.6 seconds and setting a new world record for a mile and a half on a dirt course. The winning margin was returned as 31 lengths, but, as Charlie Hatton reported, 'You couldn't find the others with two pairs of binoculars.'

It was a shattering performance, unprecedented in the annals of classic racing, and it was not over yet! So strongly was Secretariat travelling at the finish that Turcotte's efforts to pull him up were defied. With the jockey hauling back on the reins, almost standing in the stirrups, Secretariat was clocked under world record time for a mile and five furlongs!

Secretariat ran six more times, establishing his quality beyond doubt against older horses and on grass courses. He even contrived to get beaten on two occasions, once by a horse with the singularly unglamorous name of Onion. But 'Big Red' can be forgiven those lapses in the Whitney and Woodward Stakes; we all have days when we would much rather stay in bed than go to work, and Secretariat was no exception.

What is more to the point is what he was *capable* of doing. And he showed us that in the Belmont Stakes. When the stalls open for that supreme championship in the Elysian Fields, look for the blue and white blinkers. He might set them all a blistering pace from the outset, or he could come with a breathtaking surge from the rear; either way, he'll be a danger to the best of them.

And if you accept Charlie Hatton's verdict on the great chesnut's speed – 'He could not have moved faster if he had fallen off the grandstand roof' – you might just fancy your chances of backing the winner.

BELMONT STAKES. At Belmont Park, New York, USA, Saturday, 9 June 1973. 1½ miles. $90,120 to the winner. For 3-year-olds only.

Meadow Stables' ch.c. Secretariat. 9st olb	R. Turcotte	1
Elmendorf's b.c. Twice a Prince. 9st olb	B. Baeza	2
A.I. Appleton's ch.c. My Gallant. 9st olb	A. Cordero, Jr	3
C. V. Whitney's b.c. Pvt Smiles. 9st olb	D. Gargan	4
S. Sommer's b.c. Sham. 9st olb	L. Pincay, Jr	5

Winner bred by Meadow Stud. Trained by L. Laurin.

Betting: 1–10 Secretariat, 51–10 Sham, 124–10 My Gallant, 143–10 Pvt Smiles, 173–10 Twice a Prince.

Won by 31 lengths, ½ length. Time: 2min 24.0sec.

GRUNDY

*when the champion colts of successive generations gave their
all in a thrilling, uncompromising duel*

Sport in general, and racing in particular, owes a vast debt to
the Stuart monarchs. The Restoration of 1660 brought a
welcome relief from the barren years of the arch-spoilsport
Oliver Cromwell, who had been a trifle over-dramatic (and
300 years before his time) when outlawing football as a form
of riotous assembly. Charles II returned to indulge in and
promote healthy recreational activities, paying special attention
to horse racing. He rode in races himself, put up prizes to be
contested (one of the original sponsors!), and was responsible
for placing Newmarket on the map.

It was this profligate yet immensely likeable 'Merry
Monarch' who made racing the Sport of Kings, setting a family
tradition which has survived, albeit very tenuously at times,
until the present day. His niece Anne, who came to the throne
in 1702, became the Queen of Sports, revelling in the country
pursuits like hunting, driving, riding, and racing. Here was
blessed relaxation from a grief-stricken domestic life and an
official position which consisted of being the ball kicked
around by those ghastly war-mongering Whigs and frightfully
high-minded Tories.

The story goes that Anne was riding out from Ascot, where
she had previously established kennels and stables, one spring
morning in 1711, when she paused on the common and was
suddenly struck with the notion that here was the ideal setting
for a racecourse. She at once gave orders for the preparation
of a course and the *London Gazette* of July 12 announced that
races would take place on the following August 6 and 7,
including a plate of 100 guineas graciously presented by Her
Majesty.

In fact there was a little delay in the arrangements, so that
the races did not come off until August 11 and 13. It was then
that the indolence of the eminent Jonathan Swift – 15 years

before Gulliver – precluded him from assuming the dubious distinction of 'Father of Racing Journalism'. He recorded in one of his *Letters to Stella* that he had intended to be present, but that he missed all the coaches, 'and ride I would not'. Doubtless he would have given us some sort of account of those first events; the names of the runners have been preserved, but evidently nobody thought the results worth recording.

Whatever their outcome, the races proved an enormous success and there was another meeting on the new course a month later. Anne made Ascot a regular feature of the social calendar and though it lapsed for some time after her death in 1714, it was frequently revived by succeeding monarchs until, in 1768, it became firmly established. Only World Wars have prevented its celebration in every subsequent year.

To many people, of course, Ascot means Royal Ascot, the four-day festival in June attended by the Queen and many of her family. The occasion is replete with pageantry and ceremony of a kind only England, fortified by centuries of tradition, can stage convincingly. It also attracts the very best of the equine species and many of the more dreadful specimens of the human race, who attend simply because it is 'the done thing' and impair the enjoyment of the real enthusiasts.

To me, Ascot means a day in July, generally the last Saturday in that month. The Queen is there again – there is no more genuine horse lover nor a keener racegoer – and again there is a mass of humanity. But this is an occasion reserved for the true devotee of the sport, a gathering of racing aficianados from all over the world for what is almost invariably the most significant contest run on the British Turf during the year.

The race is the King George VI & Queen Elizabeth Stakes, with prize money in the region of £100,000 and a roll-call of runners which reads like an international equine *Debrett*. Here are the real aristocrats of the thoroughbred world, competing over a mile and a half for what has been described as the first leg of the World Triple Crown. (The series is completed by the Prix de l'Arc de Triomphe at Longchamp and the Washington International at Laurel). All three are open to three-year-olds and upwards, encouraging the participation of champions of different generations. The Ascot race, brainchild of the late clerk of the course, Sir John Crocker Bulteel, has not always succeeded in its ambitious aim. But the gallery of winners is graced with the figures of such as Tulyar, Pinza,

Ribot, Ballymoss, Right Royal, Ragusa, Busted, Park Top, Nijinsky, Mill Reef, Brigadier Gerard, and Dahlia. And there have been a host of internationally renowned contenders who were not good enough to win.

The renewal of 1975 produced the most stirring contest yet. Indeed, it provided what many people are inclined to regard as the finest horse race on British soil for generations. The atmosphere was electric. The principal protagonists were of the highest order. And the excitement engendered by their display of supreme class and gameness reduced strong men to tears. It was an emotion-charged moment which touched the heart of every spectator and, though we did not know it at the time, broke the hearts of both adversaries.

The hot favourite for the first prize of £81,910 was the three-year-old Grundy, undisputed champion of his generation in his first season and the winner of a Derby on each of his latest two outings. This elegant chestnut with a flaxen mane and tail carried the colours of a popular Italian doctor, Carlo Vittadini, who had bought him as a yearling for 11,000 guineas. At Epsom he had scorched home to beat the French-trained filly Nobiliary by three lengths, and he had followed up by taking the Irish Sweeps Derby with another flashing burst of pace over King Pellinore. The recent memory of those scintillating displays could only make him a firm public fancy, and he started at odds of 4–5.

The leader of the four-year-old contingent was Bustino, who raced in the familiar brown and green livery of Lady Beaverbrook. She had been the most ardent supporter of the British thoroughbred for a decade, laying out fortunes at the yearling sales with scant reward until this colt came along to provide her first classic victory in the 1974 St Leger. Overall, he had probably been the best colt of his generation as a three-year-old, and he had returned in magnificent style at four to win the Coronation Cup at Epsom. There he returned a time over two seconds faster than Grundy had recorded over the same course and distance in the Derby; indeed, his clocking of 2 minutes 33.31 seconds eclipsed every previous performance over the Epsom mile and a half. He was surely a worthy second favourite at 4–1.

The third generation to be formidably represented was the five-year-old division. The mare Dahlia had run unplaced in each of her four 1975 efforts to date, but she had won the King George VI & Queen Elizabeth Stakes in each of the two preceding seasons, also had an Irish Oaks, a Washington International, and a Canadian International Championship on her list of credits, and had closed 1974 as the world's leading stakes-winning filly. Having shown a glimpse of her old form in her previous race at Saint-Cloud, Dahlia was third best in the betting at 6–1.

Dahlia was not the only five-year-old to enter calculations, for the German-trained Star Appeal had burst upon the international scene only three weeks earlier with a remarkably facile victory in the Eclipse Stakes at Sandown Park. Add to that a previous success over Dahlia and others in the Gran Premio di Milano, and it was clear that he was a horse of considerable merit. Bedecked with his customary pair of green blinkers, Star Appeal was backed at 13–1.

Five of the other runners had proved their mettle in high-class company, most particularly Ashmore, who had also broken the Epsom course record when a close second to Bustino in the Coronation Cup, and Dibidale, heroine of the 1974 Irish Oaks. But it was the other pair, 500–1 no-hopers, who were to wield more influence on the outcome of the race. They were the five-year-old Kinglet and the three-year-old Highest, whose function was simply to guarantee a strong gallop from start to finish. They were acting on stable-mate Bustino's behalf, intending to blaze a trail so ferocious that Grundy would expend all his energy in the chase, blunting the edge of his deadly finishing pace. It was a cunning, but perfectly legitimate tactic, which had been employed successfully before, most notably in the 1949 Ascot Gold Cup, when the 'rabbits' Stockbridge and Benny Lynch had assisted Alycidon to victory over Black Tarquin. This time it did not quite work.

A long dry summer had made the Ascot going firm, conditions which were considered ideal for the Bustino camp. Trainer Dick Hern had the colt in tremendous fettle, while both pacemakers were obviously well tuned-up for their task. Grundy looked a picture of elegance as he cantered to the start. He had run in four classic races in recent weeks, winning three of them, but had continued to thrive in Peter Walwyn's skilful hands and seemed the epitome of health and fitness.

The start was delayed a little by Dahlia, who seemed less than anxious to enter her stall, but she was soon persuaded to co-operate and the starter sent the eleven representatives of three nations on their way. It had been obvious that the first colours to show in front would be those of Lady Beaverbrook, but it occasioned more than a little surprise to see that they were those worn by Joe Mercer, on Bustino, rather than those of one of the pacemakers. Mercer looked disconcerted for a few moments, glancing to his outside for his lost comrades, but the anxiety passed rapidly as Frankie Durr, on Highest, and Eric Eldin, on Kinglet, galvanised their mounts into action. Within seconds the Beaverbrook batallion formed a mighty phalanx of brown and green at the head of affairs; then, seconds later, they changed formation to race in Indian file – first Highest, second Kinglet, third Bustino.

Highest was entitled to run. Both his parents had won classic races and he had cost his owner 29,000 gns at the yearling sales. Although he had never done anything to indicate that he was worth that number of pennies, he could make handsome retribution here if he were to do his job well, and Durr ensured that he worked hard to that end. The furious gallop he set might not have worried Grundy's jockey, Pat Eddery, but there was always the daunting knowledge that when Highest dropped out, as clearly he must, there would be Kinglet to press on in his stead. With this relay team to attack him all the way, there would be no opportunity for Grundy to get a 'breather', yet he had to remain within striking distance throughout.

Mercer felt confident enough about the proceedings up front to let Star Appeal disturb the Beaverbrook monopoly in the leading positions. As Highest strode clear of Kinglet, Greville Starkey drove the German colt into third place and did so with such urgency that it seemed he might take the pacemakers on at their own game. Bustino retained fourth place, just ahead of Grundy, Ashmore, and Dahlia.

Highest's predictable collapse came at the half-way mark, where Kinglet took over the pace-setting duties. The change-over was effected fluently, with no discernible slackening of the tempo. But Kinglet was not the horse for this role. He was no better than a modest staying handicapper and he had already run three-quarters of a mile faster than had ever been required of him in the past. In his own class, he might have lasted longer; in the company of Europe's best, he was incapable of keeping them on the stretch as the situation demanded.

With half a mile to run Kinglet's tank was clearly running dry. Mercer, alive to the dangers which that might mean, acted fast, shaking the reins at Bustino and evoking an immediate response. The acceleration was smooth and sharp, an incisive burst which demolished Kinglet and Star Appeal in a couple of strides and telegraphed to Grundy, 'Now catch me if you can!'

Eddery had been anticipating Mercer's move. He had stayed commendably close to Bustino throughout, knowing that he could not allow that splendid stayer too much rope. Everything had gone according to plan until he saw Mercer press the accelerator. Then, horror of horrors, Grundy failed to respond when given the identical message.

As they came into the straight Bustino led by four lengths and seemed to have poached a winning advantage. Grundy was chasing him now, but that vital change of pace which had characterized his classic victories at Epsom and The Curragh was conspicious by its absence this time. The ploy with the pacemakers seemed to have done the trick for Bustino.

It was unthinkable that so sound a stayer as Bustino would run out of stamina, so now the issue hung on whether Grundy could call on reserves of courage as effective as the reserves of speed on which he had hitherto relied. The answer was a long time coming, so long in fact that many felt Ascot's short three-furlong straight would never end.

Riding with all the strength, energy, and skill which made him Britain's youngest champion jockey for half a century, Eddery drove Grundy closer. From the stands it seemed the older horse's race, for the gap diminished only inch by inch and Bustino was by no means stopping. Mercer, the supreme stylist who rode his first winner almost two years before Eddery was born, kept Lady Beaverbrook's colt going in perfect rhythm. It seemed unlikely that Bustino would be able to quicken again if called upon to do so – he was not that sort of horse – but it was up to Eddery and Grundy to make that necessary, and with two furlongs to go it still seemed that they could not do it.

But Eddery's frenetic driving and well-timed applications of the whip now started to pay dividends. Grundy began to develop a shade more power and the gap reduced more quickly as Bustino could only run on at the same pace. With a furlong left to run, they were level. Surely this was the end now. Grundy had only to sustain his momentum and he would go on to a hard fought, but nevertheless clear victory by about a couple of lengths.

Not a bit of it. Grundy's arrival on the scene acted only as an additional spur to Bustino, who had got too used to the idea of leading to want to surrender now. Grundy, too, had toiled hard to recover his lost ground and he refused to give way. This was a classic war of attrition, each warrior defending his colours as though life itself depended on it.

This dual display of unyielding, indomitable courage thrilled, exhilarated and intoxicated the thousands in the stands. A number were so overcome with admiration that they found themselves cheering both horses, almost in the same breath. Then, as this gripping tension seemed to be shortening the lives of spectators, came release.

With no more than fifty yards to go, Bustino had given his all. He had battled heroically under the severest pressure; now his energy ebbed suddenly away and he was beaten. Grundy was home by half a length at the end of a contest which undoubtedly revealed not one hero, but two.

The announcement of the time confirmed the status of these heroes. Grundy had lopped 2.36 seconds off the course record and Bustino, naturally, had beaten it too. At 2 minutes 26.98 seconds, this was the fastest mile and a half ever electrically recorded in Britain.

Everyone went home from Ascot with a feeling of elation that day. They had seen two great colts, both bred and trained in England, cover themselves with glory in the most keenly fought contest of class, courage, and endurance they might ever witness.

The sequels to this unforgettable occasion provided startling and distressing contrast. Bustino never ran again, suffering an apparently trifling injury during his preparation for the Prix de l'Arc de Triomphe and being retired to stud. Grundy turned out once more in the Benson and Hedges Gold Cup at York, running like a shadow of his former self to finish a long way behind Dahlia, Card King, and Star Appeal, each of whom he had trounced at Ascot. He, too, was transferred to stud.

The rigours of that gruelling Ascot battle exacted a terrible toll. Their performances that day exemplified everything understood by the term 'thoroughbred'. Unfortunately, they also brought stark reality to the old cliché, 'They ran their hearts out'.

KING GEORGE VI & QUEEN ELIZABETH DIAMOND STAKES. At Ascot, Saturday, 26 July 1975. 1½ miles. £81,910 to the winner. For 3-year-olds and up.

C. Vittadini's ch.c. Grundy. 3yrs, 8st 7lb   P. Eddery 1
Lady Beaverbrook's b.c. Bustino. 4yrs, 9st 7lb   J. Mercer 2
N.B. Hunt's ch.m. Dahlia. 5yrs, 9st 4lb   L. Piggott 3
X. Beau's b.h. On My Way. 5yrs, 9st 7lb   W. Pyers 4
R. Hakim's b. or br.h. Card King. 7yrs, 9st 7lb   R. Jallu 5
D. Wildenstein's b.c. Ashmore. 4yrs, 9st 7lb Y. Saint-Martin 6
N.J.F. Robinson's ch.f. Dibidale. 4yrs, 9st 4lb   W. Carson 7
Mrs J.G. Rogers's ch.c. Libra's Rib. 3yrs, 8st 7lb F. Morby 8
W. Zeitelhack's b.h. Star Appeal. 5yrs, 9st 7lb   G. Starkey 9
Lady Beaverbrook's b.h. Kinglet. 5yrs, 9st 7lb   E. Eldin 10
Lady Beaverbrook's b.c. Highest. 3yrs, 8st 7lb   F. Durr 11

Winner bred by Overbury Stud. Trained by P.T. Walwyn.

Betting: 4–5 Grundy, 4–1 Bustino, 6–1 Dahlia, 13–1 Star Appeal, 18–1 Ashmore, 20–1 On My Way, 33–1 Dibidale, Libra's Rib, 66–1 Card King, 500–1 others.

Won by ½ length, 5 lengths. Time: 2min 26.98sec.

CHAMPIONSHIP ROLLS

2000 GUINEAS STAKES
3-y-o Newmarket 1m

		Trainer	Jockey
1946	Happy Knight	H. Jelliss	T. Weston
1947	Tudor Minstrel	F. Darling	G. Richards
1948	My Babu	F. Armstrong	C. Smirke
1949	Nimbus	G. Colling	E. C. Elliott
1950	Palestine	M. Marsh	C. Smirke
1951	Ki Ming	M. Beary	A. Breasley
1952	Thunderhead	E. Pollet	R. Poincelet
1953	Nearula	C. Elsey	E. Britt
1954	Darius	H. Wragg	E. Mercer
1955	Our Babu	G. Brooke	D. Smith
1956	Gilles de Retz	C. Jerdein	F. Barlow
1957	Crepello	N. Murless	L. Piggott
1958	Pall Mall	C. B-Rochfort	D. Smith
1959	Taboun	A. Head	G. Moore
1960	Martial	P. J. Prendergast	R. Hutchinson
1961	Rockavon	G. Boyd	N. Stirk
1962	Privy Councillor	T. Waugh	W. Rickaby
1963	Only For Life	J. Tree	J. Lindley
1964	Baldric	E. Fellows	W. Pyers
1965	Niksar	W. Nightingall	D. Keith
1966	Kashmir	C. Bartholomew	J. Lindley
1967	Royal Palace	N. Murless	G. Moore
1968	Sir Ivor	M. V. O'Brien	L. Piggott
1969	Right Tack	J. Sutcliffe Jr	G. Lewis
1970	Nijinsky	M. V. O'Brien	L. Piggott
1971	Brigadier Gerard	W. Hern	J. Mercer
1972	High Top	B. van Cutsem	W. Carson
1973	Mon Fils	R. Hannon	F. Durr
1974	Nonoalco	F. Boutin	Y. Saint-Martin
1975	Bolkonski	H. Cecil	G. Dettori

1000 GUINEAS STAKES
3-y-o fillies Newmarket 1m

		Trainer	Jockey
1946	Hypericum	C. B-Rochfort	D. Smith
1947	Imprudence	J. Lieux	W. Johnstone
1948	Queenpot	N. Murless	G. Richards
1949	Musidora	C. Elsey	E. Britt

1950	Camaree	A. Lieux	W. Johnstone
1951	Belle of All	N. Bertie	G. Richards
1952	Zabara	V. Smyth	K. Gethin
1953	Happy Laughter	J. Jarvis	E. Mercer
1954	Festoon	N. Cannon	A. Breasley
1955	Meld	C. B-Rochfort	W. Carr
1956	Honeylight	C. Elsey	E. Britt
1957	Rose Royale	A. Head	C. Smirke
1958	Bella Paola	F. Mathet	S. Boullenger
1959	Petite Etoile	N. Murless	D. Smith
1960	Never Too Late	E. Pollet	R. Poincelet
1961	Sweet Solera	R. Day	W. Rickaby
1962	Abermaid	H. Wragg	W. Williamson
1963	Hula Dancer	E. Pollet	R. Poincelet
1964	Pourparler	P. J. Prendergast	G. Bougoure
1965	Night Off	W. Wharton	W. Williamson
1966	Glad Rags	M. V. O'Brien	P. Cook
1967	Fleet	N. Murless	G. Moore
1968	Caergwrle	N. Murless	A. Barclay
1969	Full Dress	H. Wragg	R. Hutchinson
1970	Humble Duty	P. Walwyn	L. Piggott
1971	Altesse Royale	N. Murless	Y. Saint-Martin
1972	Waterloo	J. W. Watts	E. Hide
1973	Mysterious	N. Murless	G. Lewis
1974	Highclere	W. Hern	J. Mercer
1975	Nocturnal Spree	S. Murless	J. Roe

DERBY STAKES
3-y-o *Epsom* 1m 4f

		Trainer	*Jockey*
1946	Airborne	R. Perryman	T. Lowrey
1947	Pearl Diver	C. Halsey	G. Bridgland
1948	My Love	R. Carver	W. Johnstone
1949	Nimbus	G. Colling	E. C. Elliott
1950	Galcador	C. Semblat	W. Johnstone
1951	Arctic Prince	W. Stephenson	C. Spares
1952	Tulyar	M. Marsh	C. Smirke
1953	Pinza	N. Bertie	G. Richards
1954	Never Say Die	J. Lawson	L. Piggott
1955	Phil Drake	F. Mathet	F. Palmer
1956	Lavandin	A. Head	W. Johnstone
1957	Crepello	N. Murless	L. Piggott
1958	Hard Ridden	J. Rogers	C. Smirke
1959	Parthia	C. B-Rochfort	W. Carr
1960	St Paddy	N. Murless	L. Piggott
1961	Psidium	H. Wragg	R. Poincelet
1962	Larkspur	M. V. O'Brien	N. Sellwood
1963	Relko	F. Mathet	Y. Saint-Martin
1964	Santa Claus	J. Rogers	A. Breasley
1965	Sea-Bird	E. Pollet	T. P. Glennon
1966	Charlottown	G. Smyth	A. Breasley

1967	Royal Palace	N. Murless	G. Moore
1968	Sir Ivor	M. V. O'Brien	L. Piggott
1969	Blakeney	A. Budgett	E. Johnson
1970	Nijinsky	M. V. O'Brien	L. Piggott
1971	Mill Reef	I. Balding	G. Lewis
1972	Roberto	M. V. O'Brien	L. Piggott
1973	Morston	A. Budgett	E. Hide
1974	Snow Knight	P. Nelson	B. Taylor
1975	Grundy	P. Walwyn	P. Eddery

OAKS STAKES

3-y-o fillies Epsom 1m 4f

		Trainer	Jockey
1946	Steady Aim	F. Butters	H. Wragg
1947	Imprudence	J. Lieux	W. Johnstone
1948	Masaka	F. Butters	W. Nevett
1949	Musidora	C. Elsey	E. Britt
1950	Asmena	C. Semblat	W. Johnstone
1951	Neasham Belle	G. Brooke	S. Clayton
1952	Frieze	C. Elsey	E. Britt
1953	Ambiguity	R. J. Colling	J. Mercer
1954	Sun Cap	R. Carver	W. Johnstone
1955	Meld	C. B-Rochfort	W. Carr
1956	Sicarelle	F. Mathet	F. Palmer
1957	Carrozza	N. Murless	L. Piggott
1958	Bella Paola	F. Mathet	M. Garcia
1959	Petite Etoile	N. Murless	L. Piggott
1960	Never Too Late	E. Pollet	R. Poincelet
1961	Sweet Solera	R. Day	W. Rickaby
1962	Monade	J. Lieux	Y. Saint-Martin
1963	Noblesse	P. J. Prendergast	G. Bougoure
1964	Homeward Bound	J. Oxley	G. Starkey
1965	Long Look	M. V. O'Brien	J. Purtell
1966	Valoris	M. V. O'Brien	L. Piggott
1967	Pia	W. Elsey	E. Hide
1968	La Lagune	F. Boutin	G. Thiboeuf
1969	Sleeping Partner	Doug Smith	J. Gorton
1970	Lupe	N. Murless	A. Barclay
1971	Altesse Royale	N. Murless	G. Lewis
1972	Ginevra	R. Price	A. Murray
1973	Mysterious	N. Murless	G. Lewis
1974	Polygamy	P. Walwyn	P. Eddery
1975	Juliette Marny	J. Tree	L. Piggott

ST LEGER STAKES
3-y-o   Doncaster   1m 6f 127 yds

		Trainer	Jockey
1946	Airborne	R. Perryman	T. Lowrey
1947	Sayajirao	F. Armstrong	E. Britt
1948	Black Tarquin	C. B-Rochfort	E. Britt
1949	Ridge Wood	N. Murless	M. Beary
1950	Scratch	C. Semblat	W. Johnstone
1951	Talma	C. Semblat	W. Johnstone
1952	Tulyar	M. Marsh	C. Smirke
1953	Premonition	C. B-Rochfort	E. Smith
1954	Never Say Die	J. Lawson	C. Smirke
1955	Meld	C. B-Rochfort	W. Carr
1956	Cambremer	G. Bridgland	F. Palmer
1957	Ballymoss	M. V. O'Brien	T. P. Burns
1958	Alcide	C. B-Rochfort	W. Carr
1959	Cantelo	C. Elsey	E. Hide
1960	St Paddy	N. Murless	L. Piggott
1961	Aurelius	N. Murless	L. Piggott
1962	Hethersett	W. Hern	W. Carr
1963	Ragusa	P. J. Prendergast	G. Bougoure
1964	Indiana	J. F. Watts	J. Lindley
1965	Provoke	W. Hern	J. Mercer
1966	Sodium	G. Todd	F. Durr
1967	Ribocco	R. Houghton	L. Piggott
1968	Ribero	R. Houghton	L. Piggott
1969	Intermezzo	H. Wragg	R. Hutchinson
1970	Nijinsky	M. V. O'Brien	L. Piggott
1971	Athens Wood	H. Thomson Jones	L. Piggott
1972	Boucher	M. V. O'Brien	L. Piggott
1973	Peleid	W. Elsey	F. Durr
1974	Bustino	W. Hern	J. Mercer
1975	Bruni	R. Price	A. Murray

THE GRAND NATIONAL
Liverpool   4m 856yds

		Trainer	Jockey
1946	Lovely Cottage	T. Rayson	Captain R. Petre
1947	Caughoo	H. McDowell	E. Dempsey
1948	Sheila's Cottage	N. Crump	A. Thompson
1949	Russian Hero	G. Owen	L. McMorrow
1950	Freebooter	R. Renton	J. Power
1951	Nickel Coin	J. O'Donoghue	J. Bullock
1952	Teal	N. Crump	A. Thompson
1953	Early Mist	M. V. O'Brien	B. Marshall
1954	Royal Tan	M. V. O'Brien	B. Marshall
1955	Quare Times	M. V. O'Brien	P. Taaffe
1956	E.S.B.	F. Rimell	D. V. Dick

1957	Sundew	F. Hudson	F. Winter
1958	Mr What	T. Taaffe	A. Freeman
1959	Oxo	W. Stephenson	M. Scudamore
1960	Merryman	N. Crump	G. Scott
1961	Nicolaus Silver	F. Rimell	H. Beasley
1962	Kilmore	R. Price	F. Winter
1963	Ayala	K. Piggott	P. Buckley
1964	Team Spirit	F. Walwyn	G. W. Robinson
1965	Jay Trump	F. Winter	Mr C. Smith
1966	Anglo	F. Winter	T. Norman
1967	Foinavon	J. Kempton	J. Buckingham
1968	Red Alligator	D. Smith	B. Fletcher
1969	Highland Wedding	G. Balding	E. Harty
1970	Gay Trip	F. Rimell	P. Taaffe
1971	Specify	J. Sutcliffe	J. Cook
1972	Well To Do	T. Forster	G. Thorner
1973	Red Rum	D. McCain	B. Fletcher
1974	Red Rum	D. McCain	B. Fletcher
1975	L'Escargot	D. Moore	T. Carberry

INDEX

138

141